JOHN

D0729091

Discovering
London Curiosities

SHIRE PUBLICATIONS

The cover illustration is 'A New Love Song Only Ha'penny a Piece', one of the 'Cries of London' painted by F. Wheatley RA.

British Library Cataloguing in Publication Data: Wittich, John Discovering London Curiosities. – 4th ed. 1. Walking – England – London – Guidebooks 2. London (England) – Guidebooks I. Title II. London curiosities 914.2'1'04859 ISBN 0-7478-0346-3

All photographs are acknowledged to Cadbury Lamb except those on pages 30, 36 and 73, which are the copyright of John and Andrew Wittich. The maps are by Robert Dizon using Ordnance Survey material.

Published in 1997 by Shire Publications Ltd, Cromwell House, Church Street, Princes Risborough, Buckinghamshire HP27 9AA, UK. Copyright © 1973, 1980, 1990 and 1997 by John Wittich. First published 1973; second edition 1980; third edition 1990; fourth expanded edition 1997. Number 165 in the Discovering series. ISBN 0 7478 0346 3.

Printed in Great Britain by CIT Printing Services, Press Buildings, Merlins Bridge, Haverfordwest, Pembrokeshire SA61 1XF.

CONTENTS

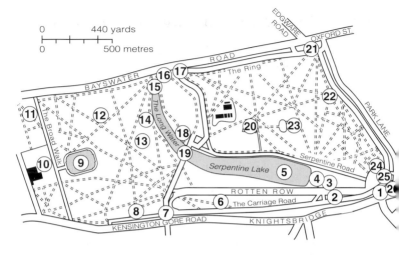

Hyde Park and Kensington Gardens

1. Decimus Burton screen
2. Life Guards memorial plaque
3. Holocaust stone
4. Dell
5. Serpentine
6. Great Exhibition site
7. Ceremonial gates
8. Albert Memorial
9. Round Pond
10. Sunken Garden
11. Elfin Oak
12. Parish boundary stones
13. William Kent's temple
14. Peter Pan's statue
15. Pumping house
16. Queen Anne's Summer House
17. Pets' Cemetery
18. Henry Moore's Arch
19. Rennie's bridge
20. Police station
21. Marble Arch
22. Joy of Life fountain
23. Children's Party fountain
24. Achilles statue
25. Queen Elizabeth Gates
26. Apsley House

1
Hyde Park and Kensington Gardens

Collectively Hyde Park and Kensington Gardens cover an area of 636 acres (257 hectares), the former royal hunting park of Henry VIII accounting for 361 acres (146 hectares) and its neighbour, Kensington Gardens, about 275 acres (111 hectares). It is difficult to distinguish their boundaries but their contents are quite different: Hyde Park has acre after acre of pleasant green 'fields' while Kensington Gardens boasts flowers beds, a boating pond and well-defined avenues of trees leading towards Kensington Palace. Originally the property of Westminster Abbey, it became Crown property at the dissolution of the abbey in 1536. Elizabeth I held military reviews in the park, and it was first opened to the public in the reign of James I, and later in the seventeenth century horse and foot races were held in it. After the triumph of the Roundheads in the Civil War all the royal parks were sold to speculators but they were reopened to the public at the Restoration of the Monarchy in 1660. Hurling matches, a combination of present-day football and all-in wrestling, were also played in the park. Samuel Pepys records in his diary coming 'finely dressed' to the parks and taking part in what has been described as a fashion parade in order to be noticed by Charles II.

When William III ascended the throne in 1689 he bought the house of the second Earl of Nottingham which was built on the edge of Hyde Park. Nottingham House, as it was then called, became Kensington Palace and about 26 acres (10 hectares) of Hyde Park became Kensington Gardens. Queen Caroline, the wife of George II, added another 200 acres (81 hectares). Queen Victoria transferred the portion of Hyde Park around the Albert Memorial to the gardens.

Lord Byron wrote of Hyde Park: 'here the fashionable fair can form a slight acquaintance with fresh air.'

Leave Hyde Park Corner underground station by Exit 3 that leads to 'Knightsbridge North Side, Hyde Park and Toilets'. Walk along to the **Decimus Burton screen (1)**, designed by Burton as a ceremonial entrance to Hyde Park. The gateway was erected in 1825. The carvings of the frieze, based on one from the Parthenon in Athens, are the work of John Herring the Younger. In the past the gateway was in constant use by horse-drawn carriages and the roadway was often covered with straw to deaden the noise, out of consideration for the patients in St George's Hospital, which used to stand where the Lanesborough Hotel is now situated.

Cross the roadway on the park side of the screen and turn left. A short way along is the **Life Guards memorial plaque (2)**, which commemorates the members of the Queen's Life Guards who were murdered on 20th July 1982 when a terrorist bomb exploded as they passed this spot. Not only soldiers, but also civilians and horses, were killed.

Now cross Rotten Row, the famous horse-riding path that once led to Kensington Palace from Westminster Palace. The complete path enables riders to circumnavigate the park and to ride for 5 miles (8 km) within the heart of London.

Further along the Row, towards the Dell, is a copse of trees. This surrounds the **Holocaust stone (3)**, which commemorates the millions of Jews sent to the gas chambers by the Nazis between 1942 and 1945. The inscription reads:

For these I weep
Streams of tears flow
From my eyes
Because of the destruction of my people.
(Lamentations)

Walk across the path from the Garden to the **Dell (4)**, a declivity surrounded by a fence. Here can be seen the Long Stone, which, according to legend, Charles I brought from Stonehenge in Wilt-

shire. In fact it is a piece of Cornish granite weighing over 7 tons which, in 1861, formed part of a drinking fountain that was subsequently removed. The Dell was laid out in the eighteenth century as a natural ruin and in the following century stones from a disused quarry, were scattered around as part of the landscape.

The path leads up to the Serpentine Road, where turn left and walk along the pathway that forms a bridge over the end of the

The memorial to the Queen's Life Guards killed by a terrorist bomb in Hyde Park in 1982.

The screen designed by Decimus Burton as a ceremonial entrance to Hyde Park.

Serpentine (5). The sinuous shape of the lake inspired its name. This stretch of water is nearly a mile in length, covers 40 acres (16 hectares) and was originally the bed of the river Westbourne that still feeds it. Any extra water required to keep the standard level is supplied from a pump on Duck Island in St James's Park. The Serpentine was created in the early eighteenth century at the instigation of Queen Caroline, the wife of George II, and took three years and the work of two hundred men to complete. Fishing is allowed in season, 16th June to the following 14th March, but only after a permit has been obtained from the superintendent's office. Boating has been allowed since the 1860s, but ice-skating is permitted only when the ice is at least 5 inches (12.7 cm) thick. Harriet Westbrook, Shelley's first wife, drowned herself in the lake in 1816 and was buried, presumably in unconsecrated ground, at St Mary's, Paddington Green, the entry in the burial register reading 'unknown person drowned in Serpentine'. From the bridge can be seen the island, which is a bird sanctuary.

One of the greatest occasions in Hyde Park was the holding of the **Great Exhibition (6)** here in 1851. The vast glasshouse, designed by Joseph Paxton, soon became known as the Crystal Palace, and after the exhibition was over the building was re-erected at Sydenham in south London, where it was destroyed by fire in 1936. The site chosen occupied an area 1843 by 450 feet (562 by 137 metres), at one end of which were two elm trees, and controversy arose as to whether they should be cut down or not. However, Paxton redesigned that part of the giant glasshouse to accommodate them. Their stumps have since been removed. The exhibition, in which exhibitors from all countries showed their industrial and artistic skills, was a brilliant success and made a profit, which was used for the establishment of some of London's great museums.

The **ceremonial gates (7)** which Queen Victoria unlocked when she officially opened the Great Exhibition now mark the boundary between Hyde Park and Kensington Gardens. They were made in Coalbrookdale, now part of the Ironbridge Gorge Museum, near Telford in Shropshire. Opening day was 1st May 1851 and the Queen was described as being 'dressed in pink watered silk, brocaded with silver and ornamented with diamonds; Prince Albert, in Field Marshal's uniform, the Prince of Wales in a kilt, and the Princess Royal was crowned with a wreath of pale-pink wild roses...'

Once described as 'an overgrown medieval reliquary', the **Albert Memorial (8)** contains the seated figure of Prince Albert, husband of Queen Victoria. Lying open on his knees is the catalogue of the Great Exhibition. Around the base of the memorial are some 180 figures depicting the arts, and in groups at the foot of the steps are the four continents. There is a story told that during the erection of the monument dinners were held on the scaffold surrounding it. Tables were laid for over eighty workmen to enjoy a menu of beef and mutton, with plum pudding and cheese to follow. The records show that although ale was offered many of the workmen were teetotallers and declined the drink. In 1990-1 the memorial was enshrouded in scaffolding in order that investigative work could be carried out to ascertain the state of the memorial. In 1995 the decorations of the structure were dismantled; some four thousand pieces were removed, barcoded and taken away from the site for cleaning and restoring. The deadline for the completion of the work is 1999. In the meantime an Albert Memorial Visitor Centre has been opened at the foot of the memorial. Here progress on the work can be checked, with several pieces of finished and unfinished sculpture on show.

The footpaths around the memorial criss-cross the southern half of the gardens and lead to the **Round Pond (9)**. Although always called the *round* pond, its shape seen from the air is like the outline of a Tudor rose. Here boys of all ages come and sail their boats, and it is recorded that the poet Shelley sailed paper boats on the pond, some made from banknotes!

On the opposite side of the Broad Walk are Kensington Palace and the **Sunken Garden (10)**, which was laid out by the Dutch William III and his wife Queen Mary as a formal garden. It was first opened to the public in 1909. The floral displays form a pleasant oasis, surrounded, cloister-like, by a Lime Tree Walk, until its destruction in the great gale of October 1987.

Walk up Broad Walk towards Bayswater Road, where, on the left-hand side, are the **Elfin Oak (11)** and children's playground. The oak originally grew in Richmond Park; the 'little people' on the oak were carved by Ivor Innes, and from the natural form of crosses, holes and indentations the artist has created a world of fairies, elves and pixies for the delight of children. The playground itself was provided by James Barrie, the author of *Peter Pan,* who, prior to the opening of the gardens to the general public, had his own private entrance and key to the grounds. He lived in a house almost opposite in the Bayswater Road. At several places in the north part of Kensington Gardens are the **boundary stones (12)** of the former Paddington Parish (PP) and the old Metropolitan Borough of Paddington (MPP).

On the opposite side of the Gardens in a slight hollow between the Round Pond and the Long Water is a perfect eighteenth-century **temple (13)**. It was designed by William Kent, the landscape architect, about 1735; Kent's skills can be seen in other places around the capital. During the late nineteenth century it 'disappeared' when extensions were added and it became part of a keeper's lodge.

The footpath that runs alongside the Long Water leads to **Peter Pan's statue (14),** designed by Sir George Frampton, which keeps alive the memory of the little boy who would not, and did not, ever grow

Model boat and owner at the Round Pond.

The statue of Peter Pan by Sir George Frampton.

up. Look for the fairy who is tiptoeing to Peter's feet, and then find the two fairies talking to the squirrel. Some of the lower figures have a distinct shine where children have patted them. The statue is said to have arrived in the Gardens when they were locked up for the night. Barrie wanted the children visiting the Gardens with their nannies to be told that during the night the fairies brought it here from the Never-Never-Land.

Continue along the path towards Bayswater Road. Here at the head of the Long Water is the former **pumping house (15)**, said to have been designed by Prince Albert; it is an imitation of the Petit Trianon at the Palace of Versailles. The house is built over the river Westbourne, which flows through three arches at the rear of the building. It forms a pleasant resting place from which to view the formal waters and flower beds at the head of the Long Water. In former times near to this spot was St Agnes Well, whose drinking water came from one of two springs here. The water from the second spring was medicinal, of euphrasian property, and a cure for sore eyes.

The pathway now rises up a slight slope passing, *en route,* **Queen Anne's summer house (16)**, built in the eighteenth century by Sir Christopher Wren for the Queen in order that she might enjoy the pleasures of the gardens. Today it serves as a resting

10

place for members of the public.

At Victoria Gate is the **Pets' Cemetery (17)**. In 1880 the Duchess of Cambridge obtained permission from Queen Victoria to bury her favourite dog here. Today there are over eight hundred little tombstones in memory of dogs, cats and birds: some are well worth reading. The key to enter the cemetery is available from the park's police station (20).

From the gate it is a pleasant walk along the pathway inside the railings of the Gardens, from where can be seen the Large Torso Arch, better known as **Henry Moore's Arch (18)**. Walk either across the grass or follow the path down to the side of the Long Water. Erected in 1980, the Roman travertine marble structure weighs 50 tons and was presented by the sculptor to the Ministry of the Environment.

A bridge **(19)** designed by Rennie in 1828 spans the end of the Long Water and the Serpentine Lake. It is the last of his London bridges still standing and is an excellent vantage point from which to view London's changing skyline. It is hard to conceive that what was once a series of 'unsightly muddy ponds' should be for us today a pleasant stretch of water on the boundary of Kensington Gardens and Hyde Park.

The Serpentine Road runs alongside the lake, where, opposite the Royal Humane Society's boat shed, there is a path leading to the **police station (20).** Police have been stationed here since 1869, as a result of a public outcry against the robberies and assaults that took place in the park.

Just beyond the police station and its adjacent Ranger's House five paths meet. Look to the left, where there is a water pump and evidence of a bath-shaped object. This was used to provide water for the sheep that used to graze the park. Take the path that leads across the grass to **Marble Arch (21)**, which once stood as a ceremonial entrance to Buckingham Palace. Designed by John Nash, George IV's favourite architect, who based it on the famous Arch of Constantine in Rome, it is built of Carrara marble and cost £100,000 (the central gates over £3000), and Chantry's equestrian statue of George IV, now in Trafalgar Square, which cost over £9000, should have been placed on top. The Arch was moved to its present site in 1851 – because, it is said, the royal coaches could not conveniently pass through! It is also a memorial to Lord Nelson and contains one of the smallest police stations in London. Maps of the eighteenth century show that a milestone stood where the Arch now stands, being the junction of two Roman roads, the Watling Street (Edgware Road) leading to Deva (Chester) and the Bayswater Road, used by the Romans to get to such places as Silchester, the West Country and south Wales. This is also Speakers' Corner, where anyone wishing to may stand on a soap-box and lecture the crowd.

On leaving Speakers' Corner walk down the avenue of trees that runs parallel to Park Lane to the **Joy of Life fountain (22).** Presented to London by the Sigismund Goetz Fund, it is the work of T. B. N. Huxley and replaced the 'Boy and the Dolphin' fountain that was exiled to Regent's Park from 1963 to 1994. The 'Boy', by Victorian sculptor Alexander Munro, has now returned to Hyde Park and can be seen in the new Rose Garden near to the Queen Elizabeth Gates.

Follow the path towards the centre of the park. After the second junction of paths is the **fountain (23)** by Theo Crosby and Polly Hope. It commemorates the International Year of the Child, celebrated in 1979. It was claimed to be the world's largest outdoor party for children: 180,000 of them celebrated the event, which was attended by Her Majesty Queen Elizabeth II. It was unveiled by Mrs Margaret Thatcher in 1981.

The path by the fountain leads down to the Serpentine Road. Turn left at the end of the road where, on a small hillock, stands the memorial of the ladies of England to the first Duke of Wellington. Usually known as the **Achilles statue (24)**, it is in fact a version by Westmacott of the horse-tamers on the Quirinal in Rome and was cast from cannon captured by Wellington's armies at Salamanca, Vittoria and Waterloo. When it was erected in 1822 a correspondent of the *Morning Herald* wrote complaining about the nudity: 'If my mother had caught any of her children looking at such an object she would have soundly whipped them.' In 1889 Friese-Green took the first recorded moving pictures, of his cousin with his son, in the vicinity.

Close by are the **Queen Elizabeth Gates (25)**, erected to serve as 'a landmark to celebrate the life and times of Her Majesty the Queen Mother'. They were designed by Giusseppe Lund with sculpture by David Wynne. They were unveiled in 1993 by Queen Elizabeth II in the presence of the Queen Mother and other members of the Royal Family. The various details on the gates reveal the interests of the Queen Mother – look for the salmon!

Today **Apsley House (26)** is the Wellington Museum, containing the Waterloo Gallery, the setting for the Waterloo dinners between 1816 and 1829, and many other items of memorabilia of the Iron Duke. Wellington's opponent, Napoleon I, was a short man, but here one can see Canova's nude statue which is more than life-size. Napoleon, it is said, disliked the statue. Apsley House was the London home of the Duke until his death in 1852, he having bought the house from his eldest brother for £42,000 in 1817.

A short walk from the house is Hyde Park Corner underground station, the starting place of the walk.

2
Green Park and St James's Park

Leave Hyde Park Corner underground station by way of the exit that leads to Knightsbridge South Side and Grosvenor Place. Here, where Knightsbridge and Grosvenor Place meet, is Hyde Park Corner, one of the busiest road junctions in London.

On the corner stands the **Lanesborough Hotel (1)**, originally built, 'on the outskirts of town', as the London home of James Lane, second Viscount Lanesborough, in 1719. Later, when Westminster Public Infirmary in Petty France was seeking to expand, two houses were offered to the governors: one close to Petty France the other at Hyde Park Corner. The choice fell on the former, but a minority of the committee favoured the latter. So it came about that the dissenters founded a new hospital in Lanesborough House. London now acquired two new hospitals, the Westminster and St George's. In recent years both hospitals have moved to new sites. The Westminster is now part of the Chelsea and Westminster in Fulham Road, SW10, and St George's is now in Blackshaw Road, SW17. The hotel is housed in the hospital building designed by William Wilkins in 1827. After the hospital moved out in 1980 the building was fully refurbished and today it is one of the most luxurious hotels in London. It advertises its presence during the night hours with lit gaseliers on the roof of the portico.

Leave the front of the hotel and walk down Grosvenor Place, cross over Grosvenor Crescent and use the subway to reach the island on which stands the Royal Artillery Memorial and the Wellington Arch.

The **Royal Artillery Memorial (2)** was designed by C. S. Jaeger and unveiled in the 1920s. It represents a howitzer of the First World War. The gun is so angled that if a shell were fired with sufficient propulsion it would land in the middle of the Somme battlefield in France, where so many gunners were killed in 1916. On the park side of the memorial look for the Blessed Virgin Mary with the Christ Child, and a container marked SRD, the latter being interpreted by old soldiers as Seldom Reached Destination. In fact it was the abbreviation for Supply Reserve Depot. Traditionally it was filled with rum!

On the opposite side of the island is the **Wellington Arch (3)**, also called the Constitution Arch and the Pimlico Arch. King George V always said his address was: 'HM The King, Buckingham Palace, Pimlico, London, SW1'.

The arch was erected as a memorial to the Duke of Wellington and was designed by Decimus Burton. Originally an equestrian statue of the Iron Duke stood on the top of the arch. This was later removed to a parade ground in Aldershot. The Quadriga sculpture by Captain Adrian Jones which is now on its roof was commissioned by Lord Michelham as a memorial to Edward VII. The small boy holding the reins of the horses is the donor's son. The figure of Peace dominates the whole structure. The arch acts as a police sub-station when required.

Leave the road island by way of the subway behind the Arch and cross to Green Park. Before entering the park, walk along Piccadilly to opposite Old Park Lane, where there stands the **porters' rest (4).** The rest is a reminder of the days when men earned their living by carrying heavy loads on their backs. Here the porter would rest his load, still strapped to his back, before continuing his journey. The inscription on the park side reads:

At the suggestion of R. A. Slaney Esq. who for 20 years represented Shrewsbury in Parliament this Porters Rest was erected in 1861 by the Vestry of St. George Hanover Square for the benefit of porters and others carrying burdens. As a relic of a past period of London's history it is hoped that the people will aid its preservation.

The porters' rest in Piccadilly.

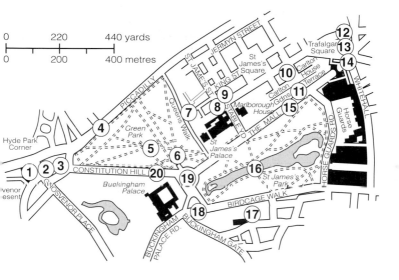

Green Park and St James's Park

1. Lanesborough Hotel
2. Royal Artillery Memorial
3. Wellington Arch
4. Porters' rest
5. Green Park
6. Canadian War Memorial
7. Passage to St James's Place
8. Lock's
9. Pickering Place
10. Athenaeum Club
11. Duke of York's Column
12. Imperial Standards
13. Nelson's Column
14. Charles I's statue
15. The Mall
16. St James's Park bridge
17. Guards Chapel and Museum
18. Plaque to Arthur Sullivan VC
19. Queen Victoria Memorial
20. Constitution Hill

Walk along Piccadilly, where the railings of Green Park are, on Sundays and bank holidays, used by artists to display and sell their works. Enter **Green Park (5)** by the first gateway and wander through one of the numerous green lungs of London. In 1767 George III, wishing to enlarge the grounds of Buckingham Palace, 'acquired' a few acres from Little St James's Park, known today as Green Park. A map of 1696 shows it as a deer park with a building in it called the Queen's Library. In the north-east corner was a reservoir belonging to the Chelsea Waterworks company. Built in 1775, it contained 1.5 million gallons (6819 cubic metres) of water. From a height of 44 feet (13.4 metres) above the high-water mark of the Thames it was possible to view the hills of Wimbledon and the Crystal Palace at Sydenham. It was filled in in 1856 but not before several persons committed suicide by drowning themselves in it.

No flowers grow in Green Park, it is said, because it is on the banks of the river Tyburn, which flows from the public execution ground. Another story was that Henry VIII, wishing to use the nearby St James's Hospice for a banquet, turned the nuns out into the snow for the night; many of the sisters died and as a result 'no flower will ever grow in the park'. To celebrate the peace of 1814 a vast Temple of Concord was erected here, with illuminations, paintings and fireworks.

The Canadian War Memorial by Buckingham Palace.

Lord Palmerston's bust in Pickering Place.

Near the Canada Gates opposite Buckingham Palace is the **Canadian War Memorial (6),** dedicated to the 1.6 million Canadians who served in the British forces in the First and Second World Wars. The Canada Memorial Foundation, in addition to raising the cost of the memorial, funds scholarships to British and Canadian universities.

From the memorial it is a short way to Queen's Walk, which runs alongside the park, and to a narrow **passageway (7)** leading to St James's Street by way of St James's Place.

At 6 St James's Street can be found **Lock's (8),** London's oldest hatters. Their window often displays historic hats, some dating back to the time of their foundation in 1793. An early customer of the shop was Mr William Coke, who asked that a hat be designed for him to wear when out hunting; when it was ready he tried it on but was dissatisfied and, putting it on the floor, jumped on it; the hat became known as the 'billycock' and was later developed into the bowler hat of today. Nearby is the shop of Berry Brothers & Rudd with an alleyway passing down the side of it. On the right is a plaque announcing that this was the office of the Republic of Texas. The inscription reads :

Texas Legation. In this building was the Legation for the Ministers from the Republic of Texas to the Court of St James 1842-1845. Erected by the Anglo-Texan Society.

Pickering Place (9) was built in the eighteenth century for a Mr William Pickering and is an unspoilt Georgian backwater of London. His mother-in-law, Widow Bourne, set up a grocery shop where now Berry Brothers' establishment is in St James's Street. The stone bust in the courtyard is of Lord Palmerston, who lived here for a time. Number 3 St James's Street is the eighteenth-century shop of Berry Brothers & Rudd, wine merchants, and successors of Widow Bourne's shop. A reminder of the widow's shop is the shop sign, two hundred years old and depicting a coffee grinder.

Turn left at the end of the street into Pall Mall and walk its length, passing a number of gentlemen's clubs until you reach the **Athenaeum Club (10),** on the corner of Waterloo Place. Outside the clubhouse is a mounting block. Whether it was made from left-over pieces of Carlton House or from the Duke of York's Steps, it was the Duke of Wellington's idea to place it here for the benefit of short men.

The mounting block by the Athenaeum Club.

At the head of the steps which lead from The Mall to Waterloo Place stands the **Duke of York's Column (11).** Frederick Augustus, Duke of York and Albany, was the second son of George III and is best remembered by the nursery rhyme 'The Grand Old Duke of York'. At the side of the steps, under a tree, is the grave of Giro, the favourite dog of the German ambassador, Hoescht, which died in 1934. The ambassador was a great friend of the Duke of Windsor, who, on Hoescht's death in 1936, ordered a British warship to take his body back to Germany.

Return to Pall Mall, turn right and walk along to Trafalgar Square. Here at the foot of the north wall can be seen the **Imperial Standards (12).** Placed there under the Act of 1876, they show the legal length of an inch, a foot, a yard, and a rod, pole or perch. The Imperial definition of an inch is that it is one-twelfth of an English or American foot. However, originally it was 'three standard ears of corn placed end to end'.

Trafalgar Square and **Nelson's Column (13)** are all part of a scheme of 1829 to commemorate Horatio, Lord Nelson (1758-1805), the column being erected between 1840 and 1843. The 185

Nelson's Column in Trafalgar Square.

foot (57 metre) column is made of Devon granite, culminating in a bronze capital, and is the work of W. Railton; the 18 foot (5.5 metre) high statue of Nelson is by E. H. Bailey, and the guardians of the column, four lions, by Sir Edwin Landseer, were placed here in 1868. Around the base on the west side a number of the stones are badly chipped. This has been pointed out as war damage – and so it is in a way, for while celebrating the Armistice of 1918 some members of the armed forces accidentally set light to a workmen's hut. The fire was so great that the heat split several of the stones – hence the damage. A move to repair them after the Second World War was rejected. The square itself was designed by Sir Charles Barry and the fountains were redesigned in 1939 by Sir Edwin Lutyens.

At the head of Whitehall stands **Charles I's statue (14)**, designed by Le Sueur. The horse's left front foot bears the date 1632, the year in which the statue was originally erected in King Street, Covent Garden. During the English Civil War it was hidden in the crypt of St Paul's church, Covent Garden, and later sold to one Rivett, who is said to have melted it down and sold the newly created pieces as souvenirs of the 'late King and martyr'. But at the Restoration of the Monarchy in 1660 it was found intact and given to Charles II, who set it up on its present site. The site of the statue had previously been occupied by the last of the Eleanor crosses. These were a number of crosses erected to commemorate the places where the body of Queen Eleanor, the first wife of Edward I, rested on its way to burial in Westminster Abbey (though her heart was buried in the Blackfriars monastery in the City). It was from this memorial cross that distances to and from London were often measured, and a bronze plaque on the pavement commemorates this. Today there is a replica of the cross on the forecourt of nearby Charing Cross railway station.

Opposite the statue is Admiralty Arch, through which can be seen **The Mall (15)**, originally laid out at the instigation of Charles II in the late seventeenth century. The avenue with four lines of trees is attributed to the designs of Andre Le Notre. Its name, and that of nearby Pall Mall, originate from *pale-maille*, a French lawn game that was played there.

Walk down The Mall and enter **St James's Park** on your left. The park covers 93 acres (42 hectares) and was first formed in the reign of Henry VIII, who walled it in as a deer park. Elizabeth I held fetes and tourneys here, while James I had an open menagerie which included everything from hawks to elephants. Charles I took his last walk through the park on his way to execution at Whitehall. Charles II, after his return from exile at the French court, asked Le Notre, the famous French landscape architect responsible for the Tuileries and Versailles gardens, to design a layout for the park, but Le Notre, it is said, refused to disturb a place of such natural

A wide avenue, The Mall, leads from Buckingham Palace to Admiralty Arch.

Feeding the birds is a favourite occupation in St James's Park.

beauty. Charles II contented himself by turning the swamps and ponds into a canal, which was later made into a lake by John Nash. The lake contains a wide variety of birds and fish but is only 4 feet (1.2 metres) deep. In winter, provided the ice is thick enough, ice-skating is permitted on it. During the First World War the lake was drained and office huts were erected in the space. Cross the lake by the **bridge (16)**, leave the park and walk to Birdcage Walk.

On the opposite side of the road can be seen and visited the **Guards Chapel and Museum (17).** The chapel was rebuilt after the Second World War, having been destroyed by a V1 flying bomb in June 1944. In the rebuilding all that was preserved from the 1834 building was the apse at the east end; the remaining portion was demolished. The new chapel presented a stark contrast to the decorated interior of its predecessor. The whiteness of the interior walls has now been relieved by the hanging of the regimental colours of the various regiments of the Brigade of Guards. The peaceful atmosphere of the chapel has to be experienced to be believed. Wonderful, too, is the music during the Sunday services, to which members of the public are welcome. Across the forecourt of the chapel, down a short flight of steps, is the Guards Museum. 'The Guards Museum was created to display the many varied and historically priceless items which are the heritage of the five Regiments of Foot Guards and to tell their story.' It is well worth a visit, but allow plenty of time – it should not be rushed!

Continue down Birdcage Walk. At the far end, on the railings of the Wellington Barracks is a plaque to Gunner **Arthur Sullivan VC (18)**. The inscription reads:

> *To the Glory of GOD and in*
> *Ever Living Memory of*
> *Gnr. ARTHUR SULLIVAN V.C.*
> *who was accidentally killed on April*
> *9th 1937 whilst serving as a*
> *representative of his country at the*
> *Coronation of H.M.King George VI.*
> *THIS TABLET WAS ERECTED BY*
> *HIS COMRADES OF THE AUSTRALIAN*
> *CORONATION CONTINGENT 1938.*

From here can be seen Buckingham Palace, the London home of the Queen. In July and August parts of the interior are opened to visitors. In front of the palace stands the **Queen Victoria Memorial (19)**. Designed by Sir Aston Webb, who also re-fronted Buckingham Palace, it stands in solitary glory at the palace end of The Mall. Built of white marble and weighing 2300 tons, it stands 82 feet (25 metres) high, with a seated statue of Queen Victoria on the east side. The sculptor, Sir Thomas Brock, shows the Queen wearing her wedding ring on her right hand in deference to her husband's continental origin. During a restoration of the statue a few years ago a workman accidentally knocked the nose of the Queen with a scaffold pole. It was repaired but the damage can still be seen! Between the memorial and the palace a pedestrianised area has been created that enables visitors to watch and photograph the changing of the guard and other ceremonial occasions without fear of traffic.

Now walk up **Constitution Hill (20)** to the right of the palace, where, it is said, Charles II used to walk his dogs for their 'constitutional'. A number of unsuccessful attempts to assassinate Queen Victoria took place on the hill and in 1850 Sir Robert Peel, founder of the Metropolitan Police Force, was thrown from his horse here. At the top is the starting place of the walk, Hyde Park Corner.

3
From Chelsea to Westminster

This walk starts at Sloane Square underground station, by the side of which is the **Royal Court Theatre (1),** the theatre where, around 1900, George Bernard Shaw's plays were first presented to London audiences, and where Ellen Terry also first appeared in a Shavian play. Originally opened in 1870 as the New Chelsea, it became the Royal Court in 1888. Over the years it has become the theatre for *avant garde* playwrights and is the home of the English Stage Company.

Sloane Square is named after Sir Hans Sloane, the noted physician whose collection of *objets d'art* was the origin of the British Museum. On the opposite side of the square to the theatre is the departmental store of Peter Jones, founded by a young Welsh draper's assistant who set up his own emporium here in 1887. The present-day building was designed by Slater, Crabtree & Moberly and was hailed at the time of its erection, 1936, as the style for the future. Alas the Second World War intervened. 'You can see it a thousand times, and it will never fail to give a little kick of exhilaration' (Ian Nairn, *Modern Buildings in London*, 1964).

Cross the square to the King's Road, originally a footpath amongst the fields but later developed into a private road for Charles II. Taken over by the local vestry in 1831, it is now Chelsea's High Street. Walk along the left-hand side of the roadway to the **Duke of York's Headquarters (2)**, built in the early nineteenth century as a school for soldiers' orphans. In 1813 the girls were transferred to Southampton and in 1909 the boys were sent to Dover. It is now used by the Territorial Army.

Continue well along King's Road to Flood Street. Turn left and walk down to the junction with Royal Hospital Road. Across the road is the entrance to **Chelsea Physic Garden (3)**, which was founded in 1673 by the Society of Apothecaries of London. It still continues its research work in botany. The gardens are open to the public on Wednesday and Sunday afternoons from April to October. Sir Hans Sloane bought the freehold and gave it to the society on condition that they would keep it 'for the manifestation of the glory, power and wisdom of God'. In 1732 cotton seeds from these gardens were sent to America, beginning the great cotton industry of that area.

A short walk from the gardens, on the site of a former monastic almshouse, theological college and military internment camp, stands the **Royal Hospital, Chelsea (4)**. It was founded by Charles II as a place of retirement for old soldiers, at the instigation of Nell

From Chelsea to Westminster

1. Royal Court Theatre
2. Duke of York's Headquarters
3. Chelsea Physic Garden
4. Royal Hospital, Chelsea
5. Ranelagh Gardens
6. River Westbourne outlet
7. Grosvenor Canal
8. Churchill Gardens Estate
9. Dolphin Square
10. Vauxhall Bridge
11. Transportation Bollard
12. Tate Gallery
13. Lambeth Bridge
14. ICI, number 9 Millbank
15. St John's, Smith Square
16. Victoria Tower Gardens
17. Jewel Tower
18. St Margaret's, Westminster

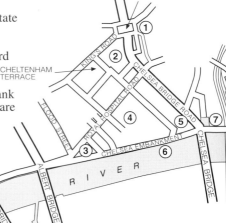

The Sunday parade service at the Royal Hospital, Chelsea.

24

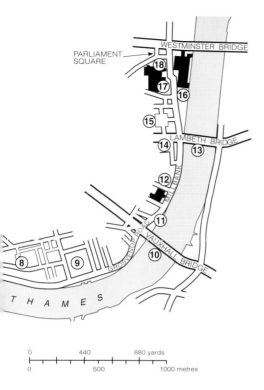

WESTMINSTER BRIDGE

(18)

(17)

(16)

(15)

LAMBETH BRIDGE

(14)

(13)

MILLBANK

(12)

(11)

GROSVENOR ROAD

VAUXHALL BRIDGE

(10)

(8)

(9)

T H A M E S

| 0 | 440 | 880 yards |
| 0 | 500 | 1000 metres |

Gwyn, and with financial help from William Sancroft, Archbishop of Canterbury, who gave £1000. The architect responsible for the design of the building was Christopher Wren. The hospital has accommodation for four hundred veterans and is open to the public daily. In the Great Hall, the refectory of the Hospital, the Duke of Wellington lay in state until his burial in St Paul's Cathedral, and a drawing in the hall shows the elaborate catafalque. Charles II's statue by Grinling Gibbons, in the Figure or Centre Court, is decked with oak leaves on the Founder's Day, 29th May, his birthday, to commemorate his escape after the battle of Worcester in 1651, when he hid an oak tree.

All that is left today of the **Ranelagh Gardens (5)**, once one of the most popular pleasure gardens in London, now forms part of the grounds of the Royal Hospital. The gardens came into being when the estates of the Earl of Ranelagh were sold and bought by speculators. The famous Rotunda, opened in April 1742, was a great success, with musical performances from early morning throughout the day. But early in the nineteenth century the public grew tired of the gardens and they were closed finally in 1805.

From the river, or from the opposite bank, can be seen the embankment aperture through which the **river Westbourne (6)** flows into the Thames. The river's source is on the west side of Hampstead and on its journey southwards it passes through Kensington Gardens (near Lancaster Gate), where it feeds into the Gardens' Long Water, and on through the Serpentine Lake of Hyde Park. When it reaches Sloane Square underground station it is channelled through an iron pipe that is visible from the platforms. It was not completely covered in until the mid nineteenth century and now forms the Ranelagh sewer.

Victoria Station stands on piles over the basin of the former **Grosvenor Canal (7)**, one of the many eighteenth-century inlets into the banks of the river. Much of the canal has been filled in today. The canal was constructed in 1725 by the Chelsea Waterworks Company. It was used by Thomas Cubitt when laying out the Pimlico estate to transport earth excavated from the docks and bricks and stone for the buildings. However, the entrance is still in use and Westminster City Council uses part of the site for the cleansing department's works.

The **Churchill Gardens Estate (8)** was designed by Powell & Moya between 1946 and 1962 and, with the Lansbury Estate in Poplar, became an architectural showpiece during the Festival of Britain of 1951. All that is left from former times is a pair of nineteenth-century public houses, the local St Gabriel's Church of England Primary School and a short row of cottage-like houses in Grosvenor Road. The estate was Westminster City Council's response to the housing problems of post-war Britain. The site is slightly over 30 acres (12 hectares); it stretches approximately 600 yards (550 metres) along the Thames at Pimlico and is 300 yards (273 metres) deep. There are 1600 flats, the blocks of which are all sited at right-angles to the river, facing west. When the flats were first erected, the space heating and domestic hot water was provided by utilising waste heat from Battersea power station on the opposite side of the river. The power station was closed down in 1983, and since that time alternative methods of supplying heat and hot water have been used.

Containing over one thousand flats, **Dolphin Square (9)** is one of the largest self-contained blocks of its kind in Europe; it is named after a nearby 'dolphin' pump used for drawing water from the river. At one time the Royal Army Clothing Department stood on this site.

The first bridge to connect Vauxhall on the south side of the Thames and Pimlico on the north was built between 1811 and

The Transportation Bollard and Henry Moore's sculpture 'Locking Pieces' at Millbank.

1815. This was replaced by the present **Vauxhall Bridge (10)** in 1906. Note in particular the larger-than-life symbolic figures on the riverside; these include Architecture holding in her hands a miniature of St Paul's Cathedral. This was the first bridge in London to carry trams over the river.

Standing at the end of a small open space on the riverside is the **Transportation Bollard (11)**, which is all that is left above ground of the Millbank penitentiary, from where prisoners were sent to Australia. The bollard was used for tying up barges alongside the riverbank. The prisoners were transferred from the barges to larger sailing ships moored in the Upper Pool of London – beyond London Bridge. An inscription on the bollard reads:

London County Council
Near this site stood Millbank Prison, which was opened in 1816 and closed in 1890. This buttress stood at the head of the river's steps from which, until 1867, prisoners sentenced to transportation embarked on their journey to Australia.

Nearby is a bronze sculpture, 'Locking Pieces', that was given to the Tate Gallery by the sculptor Henry Moore and placed here.

In the **Tate Gallery (12)**, Millbank, are the nation's collections of paintings and sculpture by British artists. It stands on part of the site of the penitentiary. Until the widening of the embankment it was possible to see the steps down which many prisoners, sentenced to deportation to the colonies, descended to be shipped abroad.

Originally there was a ferry here owned by the Archbishops of Canterbury, whose palace is nearby, but in 1862 a suspension bridge replaced it. Archbishop John Sumner received £3000 in compensation – the equivalent of 150 years rent. A painting by Leonard Knyff, in the Museum of London's possession, shows the ferry in the seventeenth century. Between 1929 and 1932 the bridge was replaced by the present **Lambeth Bridge (13)**.

Number 9 Millbank (14) was built between 1926 and 1929 for the Imperial Chemical Industries company. It was designed by Sir Frank Baines who, amongst other details, created two 460 foot (140 metre) artesian wells which were used between 1928 and 1951 to supply thousands of gallons of water. By the mid 1950s the yield had diminished and they were sealed. The 20 foot (6 metre) high main doors of the house are, in general, reminiscent of the celebrated bronze gates of the Baptistery in Florence. The doors each weigh $2^{1}/_{2}$ tons and are made of cast bronze sprayed with silveroid alloy; the panels illustrate the application of science to industry. Look for the panel showing an observatory with a man seated on the right. This is W. B. Fagan, the man who modelled the doors. The doors have no locks but are opened and closed electrically.

The next turning on the left is Dean Stanley Street and leads to **St John's church, Smith Square (15)**. The church lay in ruins for a number of years after the Second World War but has now been fully restored through the efforts of the Friends of St John's, Smith Square; although no longer a church, it is now used for concerts and recitals. Built in 1714-28 to the designs of Thomas Archer, it was one of fifty churches in and around London planned by an Act of Parliament in the early eighteenth century. When asked what type of church she would like to see here, Queen Anne is alleged to have kicked over a footstool – hence the somewhat strange design of the building with its four corner towers pointing to the sky. In *Our Mutual Friend*, Dickens describes the church as being 'like a petrified monster, frightful and gigantic on its back with its legs in the air'. However, in order to build a platform over the marshy ground on which the church stands, the towers were required to support the weight of the building, and so prevent it from sinking.

Return to Millbank, cross the roadway and enter **Victoria Tower Gardens (16)**. In the gardens are a number of interesting memorials and statues, among them the memorial to the abolitionists of slave trading in the British Empire. It originally stood in Parliament Square and is known as the Buxton Memorial Fountain. It commemorates Thomas Buxton MP, the leader of the movement. Nearer to the Victoria Tower of the Houses of Parliament stands a copy (the original is outside the Hotel de Ville in Calais) of Auguste Rodin's sculpture of 'The Burghers of Calais'. Leave the garden by the nearby gateway, passing *en route* the statue and memorial to Mrs Emmeline Pankhurst, the leader of the suffragette movement and the 'Votes for Women' campaign.

In the open space on the opposite side of the roadway is the **Jewel Tower (17)**. Its exact origin is not known for certain, but Dean Stanley, of Westminster Abbey, thought that it might have been used as a monastic prison at one time. However, the Abbey had, and still has, a small detention cell in the Dark Entry off the cloisters. Other authorities say that it was used, as its name implies, as the place where the Crown Jewels were kept, possibly on the evenings before coronations. It has been used as a depository for Parliamentary records by the Weights and Measures Department and is now an exhibition and display centre

Finally, in Parliament Square, in the shadow of Westminster Abbey, stands the church of **St Margaret's, Westminster (18)**. It is the third church on this site and dates from the fifteenth century. The east window has an interesting and curious history. Eventually, in 1758, the glass was placed in the church, but not before it had had a number of owners. Originally intended as a gift to Henry VII on the betrothal of his son Prince Arthur (Henry VIII's elder brother) to Catherine of Aragon, the daughter of Ferdinand and Isabella of Spain, it arrived in England after the deaths of both Henry VII and Arthur. The young prince kneels in the left-hand corner with St George of England his nearside companion, and Catherine of Aragon, with St Catherine of Sienna, in the opposite corner. After the execution of Sir Walter Raleigh in 1618 his headless body was buried near the high altar. His head is buried in the parish church of West Horsley in Surrey.

From Westminster underground station, opposite Big Ben, a train will return you to Sloane Square.

4
The South Bank and Victoria Embankment

Opposite Westminster underground station and standing at the foot of Westminster Bridge is the statue of **Queen Boadicea (1).** The red-headed queen (now more correctly called Boudicca) stands, with her two daughters, on a chariot, with its sharp blades projecting from the hubs of the wheels. The work of Thomas Thornycroft, it was erected in 1902, over a thousand years after she had laid to waste Roman Colchester (Camulodunum) and London (Londinium).

At the foot of the steps on the river side of the statue can be seen the **High Tide House (2),** which records the height of the river at Westminster Bridge.

Return up the steps and walk across the bridge to the south side, where can be seen the **Coade stone lion (3)**, which originally stood on the Lion Brewery. When the brewery was demolished in 1951 to make way for the Festival of Britain exhibition, the lion was used at the entrance to Waterloo Station. When it was moved,

The Coade stone lion originally stood on the Lion Brewery.

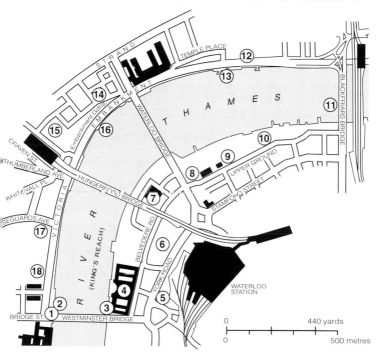

The South Bank and Victoria Embankment

1. Boadicea's statue
2. High Tide House
3. Coade stone lion
4. Former County Hall
5. General Lying Hospital
6. Shell Building
7. Royal Festival Hall
8. Royal National Theatre
9. London Television Centre
10. Gabriel's Wharf
11. Blackfriars Bridge
12. City of London dragons
13. HQS Wellington
14. Savoy Place
15. York House Watergate
16. Cleopatra's Needle
17. Whitehall Palace steps
18. Scotland Yard

several items of interest were found in a recess in the lion's back. They included two coins from the time of William IV and a trade card of the Coade family, who manufactured this artificial stone. After the festival the lion was moved to its present site and a 1966 coin and a copy of *The Times* for 17th March 1966 were added to the original items. A copy of an article in *The Times* of 5th March 1966 by J. H. Holroyd on Coade stone was also included. The plaque fixed to the plinth on which the lion stands bears the following inscription:

> *This lion, modelled by W. F. Woodington and made of Coade's Artificial Stone, stood from 1837 on the parapet above the river front of the Lion Brewery, Lambeth. It survived the surrounding devastation in the war of 1939-45, and when the site was cleared for the building of the Royal Festival Hall, was preserved in accordance with the wishes of His Majesty King George VI.*

Along the riverside nearest to the lion is the former **County Hall of London (4)**, which housed the largest municipal authority in the world until the dissolution of the Greater London Council in 1986. It has now been converted into flats and apartments. The ground here was once known as 'Pedlar's Acre' after a pedlar who bequeathed the land to the parish of St Mary Lambeth. One version of the story is that the pedlar and his dog were sheltering from a storm in the porch of the church and were both invited in to vespers; the man later considered this the turning point of his life and as a thank-offering gave the plot of land. Another story tells how the pedlar and his dog were sheltering near the ferry and the dog unearthed a treasure, and from his new-found wealth the pedlar gave the acre, or, alternatively, that the bequest was made in order that the pedlar's dog could be buried in the churchyard.

Four centuries later the London County Council purchased the land from the parish for £81,000, but as the parish vestry had been superseded by the Lambeth Borough Council it was to the latter that the money was eventually paid. A Roman boat was found when digging the foundations of the hall and is now in the possession of the Museum of London, London Wall. The architect of the riverside buildings of County Hall was Ralph Knott. The Hall opened in 1922 but much of the present complex is more recent. Part of it now houses the London Aquarium, opened at Easter 1997.

Turn away from the lion and walk down the side of the building. Shortly, on the left, is a private roadway that leads to the main entrance of the former County Hall. Here are plaques relating to the building.

Leave the area by walking under the archway opposite the main entrance, where, on the opposite side of the road, is the **General Lying Hospital for pregnant married women (5).** Founded by

John Leake, eminent writer on the diseases of women, in 1765, it was one of the largest and earliest maternity hospitals dating from the eighteenth century. A marriage certificate had to be produced before entry was allowed to the hospital for the birth of a child. A similar foundation, only for unmarried women, was founded in the Bayswater Road, near Marble Arch.

To celebrate the centenary of the Great Exhibition of 1851 in Hyde Park, the Festival of Britain was held in 1951. Bordered by County Hall on the west side and Waterloo Bridge on the east, the festival site, now known as South Bank, was developed into a cultural centre. The immense tower block of the **Shell Petroleum Company (6)**, completed in 1962, is 351 feet (107 metres) high and was designed by Sir Howard Robertson RA and his partner R. Maynard Smith and built between 1957 and 1962 by Sir Robert McAlpine & Sons Ltd. It stands on a $7^1/2$ acre (3 hectare) site and when built was the largest office building in Europe.

In 1769 the Coade family set up business on the site now occupied by the **Royal Festival Hall (7)**. Their artificial stone was both cheap and durable; the formula was based on a patent of 1722 and was used by two other 'men of Lambeth' but needed the added 'something' of the Coade family. The secret died with the family and all attempts at analysis over the years have been in vain. A grinding-stone, found in 1951, is now displayed on the river-front side of the hall on the lower level. Ironically, Coade stone has

The Royal National Theatre on the South Bank.

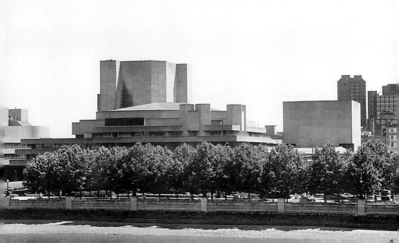

stood up to the atmosphere of London better than any natural stone. Examples can be seen in the keystones of the houses in Queen Anne's Gate, near St James's Park underground station.

On the other side of Waterloo Bridge is the **Royal National Theatre (8)**. Designed by Sir Denis Lasdun and opened by Queen Elizabeth II in 1976, it was the last part of a saga that had lasted from 1848 when the idea of a national theatre was first conceived. The building contains three separate theatres: the Olivier open-stage amphitheatre (named after the National's first artistic director, Lord Olivier), the Lyttelton (named after the National's first chairman, the English industrialist and politician Oliver Lyttelton, first Viscount Chandos) and the Cottesloe studio theatre (named after the first chairman of the South Bank Board, Lord Cottesloe). The complex includes places to eat and drink, exhibition foyers open to the public and a bookshop.

A short distance from the theatre in Upper Ground are the studios and offices of **London Television Centre (9),** housed in a building that overlooks the river Thames. The Centre is responsible for the *London Tonight* and *London Today* programmes.

Further along the road is **Gabriel's Wharf (10)**, housing a thriving community of working artists, with restaurants and sandwich bars offering refreshment for the walker or the theatregoer. During the summer months there are occasional exhibitions and displays by up and coming designers. The former Oxo building has been converted into a complex of studios, cafes and restaurants as well as a place to enjoy the spectacular views of the City and the river. In former days commentators on the pleasure boats on the Thames would always refer to the Oxo building as the only place in London where one could get a square meal for a penny – the price of an Oxo cube (used for making gravy)!

The road to the left of the wharf continues to the foot of **Blackfriars Bridge (11)**. Walk over the bridge, using the pavement on the left-hand side. On reaching the other side of the river turn left and walk along the Victoria Embankment.

Marking the boundary between the cities of London and Westminster are the columns on which are mounted the **dragons (12)** of the City of London. Although the original dragons first appeared in the armorial bearings of the City in 1609 the idea of mounting dragons at the City's boundaries dates only from 1963. In that year a bronze dragon was cast and placed on the top of the Temple Bar Memorial at the Westminster end of Fleet Street. These dragons were originally over the entrance to the City of London Coal Exchange. An inscription on the column nearest the Temple's railings reads:

These dragons represent a constituent part of the armorial

*bearings of the City of London and have been erected to indicate
the western boundary of the City. This commemorative plaque
was unveiled by the Rt. Hon. the Lord Mayor Sir Ralph Edgar
Perring on 16th October 1963. The dragons were formerly
mounted above the entrance of the City of London Coal
Exchange which was demolished in 1963.*

(On the back of the shields there can be seen the name of the
foundry that made them: Dewer London 1849.) The idea was so
popular that dragons can now be seen at all of the entrances to the
City.

Across the roadway from the river, on the railings of the Temple,
is a stone memorial commemorating the last time that Queen
Victoria came to the City in March 1900. As is the custom when a
monarch visits the City, the Lord Mayor, Alderman Frank Green,
presented her with the City Sword, which she touched and returned
to his safe keeping.

Moored, permanently, just outside the boundary of the City of
London is **HQS Wellington (13)**, now the livery hall of the
Honourable Company of Master Mariners. Formerly a sloop of the
Royal Navy, it was purchased by the company in 1947 with money
subscribed by members of the company, and moored here in the
following year. The staircase leading down to the hall, once the
engine room of the vessel, was part of the former Isle of Man and
Clyde trading ship *Viper*. The hall is not generally open to members of the public.

It is now a pleasant walk along the riverside, under Waterloo
Bridge, and across the roadway, to the building on the corner of
Savoy Place (14) and Savoy Hill which has the following inscrip-
tion:

The sloop 'Wellington' is now the livery hall of the Master Mariners.

The York House Watergate was designed by Inigo Jones.

BBC
From 1923 to 1932 the studios and offices of British Broadcasting Company and its successor the British Broadcasting Corporation were in this building.

Enter the Embankment Gardens by way of the nearest gate and walk along to the **York House Watergate (15)**, which stands marooned from the river it was built to serve. Originally the riverside entrance to York House, it was designed by Inigo Jones, with carvings by Nicholas Stone, and has stood here since the early seventeenth century.

A flight of steps beside the watergate leads to Buckingham Street. Number 15, where both Charles Dickens and David Copperfield lodged, has gone but a plaque marks the house to which the diarist Samuel Pepys came in 1679 after fire had destroyed his house in Seething Lane, near the Tower of London.

On the opposite side of the Victoria Embankment stands **Cleopatra's Needle (16)**, which in spite of bearing that illustrious queen's name has nothing to do with her except that it stood outside her palace in Alexandria! A present to England by Mehemet Ali, Viceroy of Egypt, in 1819, it did not arrive in London until

1878, when it was finally erected here. Its interesting history and the story of its voyage from Egypt are clearly told on the base of the column. The pedestal contains a time-capsule with a copy of Bradshaw's railway timetable, a Holy Bible and several newspapers of the time as well as coins of the period. The granite monolith stands 68½ feet (21 metres) high, dates from *c*.1450 BC and was originally one of a pair erected by Thothmes III outside his palace at Heliopolis. The two bronze male sphinxes at the base were designed by G. Vulliamy and modelled by C. H. Mabey.

Continue to walk along the riverside, under the Hungerford foot and Charing Cross railway bridge, to Horse Guards Avenue. Cross the roadway to the gardens, where can be seen **Whitehall Palace steps (17)**. They are all that remains of the riverside terrace built by Sir Christopher Wren in 1691 for Queen Mary, wife of William III. The plaque describes them as being 'Queen Mary's Steps', left uncovered when the tall office block behind them was being erected for the Ministry of Defence in 1957.

At the other end of the gardens is the former **New Scotland Yard (18)**, built as the headquarters of the Metropolitan Police Force on reclaimed land following the building of the Victoria Embankment in the nineteenth century. The land had previously been allocated for the building of a new national opera house and a

One of the two bronze sphinxes that guard Cleopatra's Needle.

foundation stone was laid in 1875. Due to the lack of funds the theatre was never built, but the foundations were used by the police on which to erect their building. The architect, Norman Shaw, is portrayed on the river front of the building, built of the finest granite from the quarries of Dartmoor, where the prisoners from the nearby prison were engaged to work the stone. Up to 1967 it was used as the main offices for the police until they moved to new offices in Victoria Street.

Close by is the entrance to Westminster underground station, where this walk began.

The Merchant Navy war memorials in Trinity Square.

5
The City's riverside

Immediately outside Tower Hill underground station is **Trinity Square (1)** and on the far side of the gardens is the site of the scaffold, marked today by a cobbled surface. Around three sides of the site are the names of some of the famous, and infamous, persons from the hundreds of men and women who have been publicly executed here. The first of the inscribed names is Simon of Sudbury, the Archbishop of Canterbury who was beheaded by Wat Tyler, the insurrectionist, in 1381, after being dragged from the Tower of London by the rebels. For his part in the Jacobite Rising of 1745 Simon Fraser, Lord Lovat, was executed in 1747 – the last public beheading on Tower Hill. Stands were erected surrounding the site for the many spectators who wished to witness the executions. On one occasion the stands were overcrowded and collapsed with loss of life. The prisoner was returned to the Tower until the stands were repaired and the execution could be carried out without interruption.

Also in the gardens are two Merchant Navy war memorials: the one nearest the roadway commemorates the First World War and was designed by Sir Edwin Lutyens, and the other the Second World War by Sir Edward Maufe.

Leave the gardens by the nearest gateway and cross over the roadway where, at the end of Muscovy Street, in the middle of the road can be seen the **boundary mark (2)** of the Liberty of the Tower of London. The Tower of London is outside the jurisdiction of the Lord Mayor of London and of any local borough council's authority. The governor is a direct appointment of the Crown, and as such is responsible to the monarch for the well-being of the Tower. The area surrounding the Tower is a liberty (free area) outside the City wall.

Across the road from the gardens is the parish church of **All Hallows by the Tower (3)**, dating back to Saxon times. As a result of bombing in the Second World War, a Saxon arch was uncovered in the crypt, only open to members of the public when a member of staff is available to conduct a visit, and there are the remains of a Roman villa on the site.

At the foot of Tower Hill stands the **Tower Subway Kiosk (4)**, which in 1869 was the entrance to London's first railway under the Thames: the journey took a few minutes from here to the outlet in Southwark. With the opening of Tower Bridge in 1894 the subway became redundant although it was used by pedestrians for a short time. Today it houses cables and other lines of communication.

The Subway Kiosk by Tower Hill was once the entrance to London's first railway under the Thames.

Lower Thames Street leads to the **Custom House (5),** the site of a near tragedy for English literature. Here the poet William Cowper tried to drown himself in the river – but the tide was out at the time! HM Customs and Excise is probably the oldest law enforcement organisation in the world. The earliest record of the collecting of a customs duty is AD 743 and the service has continued ever since that time. Over the years the organisation has had to collect a number of strange taxes including those on windows, hats, hair powder, fish, gloves and even vinegar. The building is not open to the general public for sight-seeing.

Just before London Bridge stands the parish church of **St Magnus the Martyr (6)**, in whose churchyard (west of the tower) can be seen stones from the medieval and nineteenth-century bridges. Records show that during the fourteenth century the Pope appointed several rectors to the living: an instance that is unique in the parochial records of the City of London.

On the other side of London Bridge from the church is the livery hall of the **Worshipful Company of Fishmongers (7),** one of the Great Twelve Companies of the City, and rated fourth in the order

40

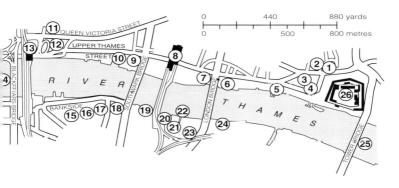

The City's riverside

1. Trinity Square
2. Boundary mark
3. All Hallows by the Tower
4. Tower Subway Kiosk
5. Custom House
6. St Magnus the Martyr
7. Fishmongers' Hall
8. Cannon Street station
9. Vintners' Hall
10. Queenhithe
11. Baynard's Castle
12. BT Museum
13. Blackfriars Station
14. Blackfriars Bridge
15. Bankside power station
16. Wren's house
17. Globe Theatre
18. Ferryman's seat
19. Anchor public house
20. Clink Prison exhibition
21. Banqueting house ruins
22. St Mary Overies Dock
23. Southwark Cathedral
24. London Bridge City
25. Tower Bridge
26. Tower of London

of precedence, having received its first charter in 1272. A guild existed long before any grant of charter: it was formed to regulate and support the fish trade of the City. Among the many exhibits in the hall is a chair made from wood of the medieval London Bridge. In a cabinet there is the dagger with which William Walworth, a member of the Company and Mayor of London, stabbed to death the rebel Wat Tyler in 1381. The hall is not generally open to members of the public but 'open days' are held during the summer months. Further information and tickets are available from the City Information Centre in St Paul's Churchyard South.

Cannon Street station (8) is on the site of the Steelyard (a corruption of the word *stapel-hof*, meaning 'heap of merchandise'), where the Easterlings, north German Baltic coast merchants, set up business between the tenth and sixteenth centuries. Also known as the Hanseatic League, they gave Britain the word 'sterling' to denote value.

Further along Upper Thames Street is the livery hall of the **Worshipful Company of Vintners (9)**, another of the Great Twelve Companies, and rated eleventh in the order of precedence. The hall, except the court room, was destroyed in the Great Fire and rebuilt in 1671. Commemorating an occasion in the fourteenth century when five kings sat down at their banquet (the monarchs of England, Scotland, France, Cyprus and Denmark), the loyal toast at the annual Feast of the Five Kings dinner is cheered five times instead of the normal three. In 1935 the four sons of King George V were entertained by the Company at the Feast. With the Dyers' Company the Vintners share the privilege of owning swans on the Thames; every July the two companies go 'swan-upping'– catching the young cygnets and marking their beaks with one notch for the Dyers' birds, two for the Vintners'. All unmarked birds belong to the Queen. This ceremony is also the origin of the inn sign the 'Swan with the Two Necks', which should be 'two nicks', although a two-headed swan is shown over the entrance to the hall in Upper Thames Street.

One of the oldest hithes (inlets on the riverbank where goods could safely be unloaded), **Queenhithe (10)** was first used in Roman times but later abandoned by larger craft, because the narrow piers of London Bridge made it impossible for them to pass into the upper reaches of the Thames. In the twelfth century it was primarily used by the Hanseatic League.

Cross over Upper Thames Street by way of the footbridge that leads to Huggin Lane and Queen Victoria Street, passing, or taking a rest in, the Fred Cleary Gardens. Cross the roadway and walk down, passing the Church of St Nicholas Cole Abbey on the right, to the **Baynard's Castle public house (11).** Baynard was one of the knights who came from Normandy with William the Conqueror. He built himself a castle on a site by the riverbank where the inn now stands. At the beginning of the thirteenth century it came into the possession of Robert Fitzwalter, the hereditary banner-bearer of the City of London, and because he sided with the barons against King John at the sealing of Magna Carta in 1215, it was destroyed. With the coming of the Dominicans (Black Friars) in the late thirteenth century the castle was moved to the river's edge to a site near the Mermaid Theatre. During the redevelopment of the area in the 1970s much of the vicinity was excavated, revealing new information about the castle; the movable fragments are in the possession of the Museum of London in the Barbican.

Across the roadway, in an office block, is the **BT Museum (12)** with its permanent exhibition 'The Story of Telecommunications'. The museum is open Mondays to Fridays (except bank holidays) from 10 am to 5 pm with a special Saturday opening for the Lord Mayor's Show in November.

Leave the museum and walk over the footbridge to the upper booking hall of **Blackfriars railway station (13)**, now entirely rebuilt on its original site. The intriguing façade has not been replaced but the former entrances have been built into the wall just outside the platforms. Here can be seen such enticing names as St Petersburg, Vienna, Wiesbaden and Berlin, but it has been a long time since one could book to these places from here.

Descend to ground level by using the escalators, turn right, and

Bankside power station from Blackfriars Bridge.

at the entrance to the station turn left and walk along to **Blackfriars Bridge (14)**. Queen Victoria laid the foundation stone of the bridge in 1865, when the present structure replaced the original eighteenth-century bridge. From one of the abutments, lovingly called 'pulpits' from their design, can be seen the stone pillars that once supported railway lines from Blackfriars railway station.

Walk across the bridge and at the far side descend to the embankment, turn right and walk along to the **Bankside power station (15)**. Designed by Sir Giles Gilbert Scott, the power station was operational from 1963 to 1980, when it was closed. It has now become a 'listed building', that is, one worthy of retention for the future, and is to be converted to house the Modern Art Collection from the Tate Gallery on Millbank.

A pleasant walk along the riverside brings one to **Wren's house (16)**. Although the present building, externally at least, is later than Wren's time it is conceivable that he lived on Bankside in the late seventeenth century when so much of his time was devoted to plans for rebuilding the City, but there is no documentary evidence to support the claim. However, there is a plaque stating 'Here lived Sir Christopher Wren during the building of St Paul's Cathedral ...' and also referring to the residence of Catherine of Aragon, the first queen of Henry VIII.

The house's new neighbour is the **Globe Theatre (17)**, the inspiration of the late Sam Wanamaker, whose dream was to re-create an exact copy of the Globe Theatre in which William Shakespeare's plays were produced and performed during the sixteenth and seventeenth centuries. It has been designed as the centrepiece of the International Shakespeare Globe Centre, 'an entertainment, educational and cultural complex'. Its thatched roof is the first to be constructed, and allowed, in London since the Great Fire of London in 1666.

On the corner of the Bear Gardens, set into the wall of the building, is the **ferryman's seat (18)**, used by the ferryman while waiting for a return trip back to the City of London. Many people, including Elizabeth I, refused to cross the river by way of London Bridge. It was considered to be too dangerous, with footpads and street muggers operating on it.

The riverside walk continues under Southwark Bridge to Bankside where the **Anchor public house (19)** stands. This was one of the favourite haunts of both William Shakespeare and Dr Samuel Johnson – but not at the same time! The building, often visited by Shakespeare between acts while his plays were being performed at the nearby Globe Theatre, was burnt down in 1676, to be replaced by the present one. Records show that originally it was called the 'Hope upon the Castille' and it was from this vantage

(Left) The ferryman's seat on Bankside and (right) the ruins of the banqueting house of the Bishops of Winchester.

point that Londoners in both the seventeenth and twentieth centuries have watched fire destroy much of the City.

Clink Street opposite the Anchor leads under a railway bridge to the site of the **Clink Prison (20)**, where today there is an exhibition set up 'underneath the arches'. The prison formed part of the Bishops of Winchester's complex here in medieval times. The prison was mainly used to house heretics and other offenders against the Church.

Another reminder of the previous occupants of the area is the ruins of the Bishops' **banqueting house (21)**, dating from the time when Southwark was part of a much larger diocese of Winchester and the Bishops entertained here in their palace.

Close by is **St Mary Overies Dock (22)**, another of the ancient hithes of London, where, since the sixteenth century, parishioners of St Saviour's, Southwark, have been entitled to land goods free of toll. The suffix 'Overy' or 'Overie' is said to have derived from 'over the river' – a medieval title differentiating Southwark's church dedicated to St Mary from the others. It could also commemorate a ferryman named Overie who plied for business along this stretch of the river. In order to find out the true feelings of his family towards himself, and to ascertain whether one of his daughters would marry a certain man of whom her father did not approve, he feigned death. His family were so pleased that, after having laid him in his coffin complete with shroud, they proceeded to have a party in the next room. Overie was not amused at the event and promptly left his coffin and entered the room where the jollifications were taking place. The daughter's boy-friend, seeing what he thought was a ghost, struck out at the advancing figure – who promptly fell down dead; this time, after they once again laid him out in his coffin, he stayed there, and the party resumed. But the daughter was so full of remorse that she entered the local convent and lived there for the rest of her life.

Permanently moored in St Mary Overies Dock is the *Golden Hind,* an exact replica of the ship in which Sir Francis Drake circumnavigated the world between 1577 and 1580. The replica was built in Appledore, North Devon, for the bicentenary exhibition of the city of San Francisco in 1977, after which it sailed around the coast of the United States of America. In 1981 it returned to England and an educational programme was set up to enable children to sample life aboard a sixteenth-century ship. It continues to be used for educational purposes and parties of school-children can spend time living on the ship as members of the crew or passengers. At other times the ship is open to the general public for a small fee.

Founded originally as St Mary-over-the-River – St Mary Overie – the present-day **Southwark Cathedral (23)** became a parish church after being an Augustinian priory for over four hundred years, and in 1905 it was raised to the dignity of a cathedral. John Harvard, founder of Harvard University in the USA, was baptised here; today St John's Chapel is known more popularly as the Harvard Chapel and is maintained by the university. The stone screen behind the high altar is virtually a history book in stone with the figures representing persons connected with Southwark and the Church through the ages. In the entrance to one of the vestries can be seen a very rare twelfth-century consecration cross, inscribed there in 1107. For the Shakespeare enthusiast the modern stained glass window above the memorial to the Bard will provide him, or her, with a chance to test their knowledge of Shakespeare's plays.

On the other side of London Bridge from the cathedral is **London Bridge City (24)**, made up of restored and rebuilt warehouses along the river front. The centrepiece is Hay's Galleria, taking its name from Hay's Wharf of earlier times. It was in 1651 that a certain Alexander Hay set up a wharf here, thus making it the

Bishop Fox's screen in Southwark Cathedral.

oldest surviving wharf of the Port of London. Stretching from London Bridge to Tower Bridge, it is also the longest wharf. As early as 1867 the wharf was a pioneer in installing a cold storage plant where New Zealand butter and cheese could be safely stored. In 1931 the warehouse was rebuilt as offices to the designs of H. S. Goodhard-Rendel and the building is now listed. Hay's Wharf today is an experience to be enjoyed, with breathtaking views across the river, and with shops, cafes, bars and restaurants to entice visitors.

At the end of the riverside walk is **Tower Bridge (25)**. Opened in 1894 by the then Prince of Wales, later Edward VII, it forms a magnificent 'gateway' to the City of London. The upper levels of the bridge have been converted into an exhibition showing the history and development of the bridge and the river. From the enclosed upper walkway there are magnificent views over London that have to be seen to be believed.

Finally there is the **Tower of London (26)**, itself dominated by the great White Tower in the centre of what is really Her Majesty's Royal Palace and Armouries of the Tower of London. Actually outside the City of London, it is a perfect example of a concentric castle. Tower Hill underground station, where the walk began, is close by.

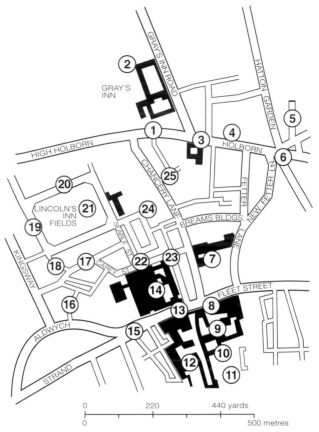

Lawyers' London

1. Cittie of York
2. Gray's Inn
3. Holborn Bars
4. Site of Furnivall's Inn
5. Bishop of Ely's palace
6. Statue of Prince Albert
7. Public Record Office
8. Prince Henry's Room
9. Temple church
10. Crown Court Row
11. Inner Temple gardens
12. Middle Temple Hall
13. Temple Bar

14. Royal Courts of Justice
15. St Clement Danes
16. Clare Market
17. Portugal Street
18. 'Old Curiosity Shop'
19. 59-60 Lincoln's Inn Fields
20. Sir John Soane's Museum
21. Execution plaque
22. Sir Thomas More statue
23. Carey Street boundary stones
24. Lincoln's Inn Chapel
25. London Silver Vaults

6
Lawyers' London

From Chancery Lane underground station it is a short walk along High Holborn to the **Cittie of York public house (1)**, which stands by the entrance to Gray's Inn.

A tavern was first established on the site of the Cittie of York in 1430 and from 1695 to 1984 it was Henekey's Wine House. It has since been taken over by Samuel Smith's brewery and given its current title. The present building has extensive cellars, which were put to good use as shelters in the times of the anti-Catholic Gordon riots of the eighteenth century. Dickens has David Copperfield in temporary residence in the gatehouse next door to the tavern. A triangular fireplace in the centre of the room appears to have no chimney; the smoke escapes from the fireplace by way of a chimney under the floor. For those who wish to test their prowess at drinking, a yard-glass is available. It holds 3.75 pints (2.13 litres) and all one has to do is drink the contents down in one go without pausing for breath or spilling any.

The entrance to **Gray's Inn (2)** is through the gatehouse near to the tavern and leads into another world. Founded in the fourteenth century the Inn occupies land where the mansion of Lord Grey de Wilton once stood. After his death in 1308 the property was left vacant until the Society of Gray's Inn was formed. One tree in the garden is said to have been planted by Sir Francis Bacon, who laid out the gardens in the seventeenth century. The gatehouse, first built in 1594 and rebuilt in 1964-65, makes a worthy entrance to this quiet backwater of learning. Shakespeare's *Comedy of Errors* was first performed in the hall of the Inn in 1594. The public are free to wander the grounds, providing they do not make a nuisance of themselves, nor enter any building without permission.

Leave the Inn by way of the gatehouse that leads into Gray's Inn Road, turn right and return to Chancery Lane underground station.

At the junction of Gray's Inn Road and Holborn stands **Holborn Bars (3)**, one of a series of outer 'gates' set some distance from the City walls. They were not fortified gates, more like the bars at frontier posts where tolls and commercial dues could be collected. The keepers of the bars could also scrutinise persons entering the city and perhaps turn away those who were suffering from a contagious disease. In recent times a 'ring of steel' has been set up around the outer perimeters of the City to prevent the infiltration of terrorists. Opposite the dragons, marking the boundary of the City, stands Staple Inn.

An 'inn', strictly interpreted, is a place where lodgings, as well as food, can be had. In the fourteenth century the wool staplers (wool merchants) settled at Holborn Bars and, naturally, their inn became Staple Inn. Today the front presents a glimpse of London of the late middle ages. In order to pay for his mother's funeral Dr Samuel Johnson, who lived here between 1759 and 1760, wrote *Rasselas.* The Institute of Actuaries now uses part of the building as its offices. The hall is not open to the public.

The site of the former **Furnivall's Inn (4),** is now occupied by the Prudential Assurance Company's offices, designed by Alfred Waterhouse. Charles Dickens had chambers here from 1834 to 1837 but when his first child was born he and his young wife, Catherine Hogarth, moved to 48 Doughty Street.

Walk along Holborn, past Hatton Garden, to Ely Place, where in the thirteenth century the Bishops of Ely built a **palace (5)** for

The half-timbered Staple Inn in Holborn.

themselves, comprising a very fine complex of rooms. The land is extra-parochial as far as the rest of London is concerned, having its own beadle to maintain order. Prior to the Second World War the beadle used to patrol the street and called out the state of the weather and the time of night: 'Twelve of the clock on a misty night, and all's well.' The gates at the entrance are still locked every night, and no policeman patrols the street, only entering if specifically requested to do so. The chapel of the former palace is now a Roman Catholic church and is normally open during the day.

Return to the roundabout at Holborn Circus and London's politest statue, the equestrian statue of **Prince Albert (6).** The seated figure of Queen Victoria's consort always raises his hat to passers-by. Sculpted by Charles Bacon, it was erected in 1874 at a cost of £2000. Around the base can be seen plaques showing the prince laying the foundation stone of the present Royal Exchange in 1842, and another showing Britannia distributing 1851 Great Exhibition awards. At either end of the base there are statues of Commerce and Peace.

From the roundabout walk down New Fetter Lane and at the junction with Fetter Lane cross over to Breams Buildings, which leads to Chancery Lane. Here is the **Public Record Office (7)**, established by an Act of Parliament of 1838, before which time the national records and archives were stored in the Tower of London. Since the building of the office – the Fetter Lane side dates from 1851-66 – a unique collection of documents relating to the history of Britain has been housed here, ranging from the Domesday Survey of 1086 to parliamentary writs and returns. The office, one of the least visited museums in London, has much in it to interest the curiosity hunter. (To accommodate the growth of archival material of recent date a new store was opened in 1977 at Kew.)

At the end of Chancery Lane is Fleet Street and here can be found, and visited, mornings only, Monday to Friday, **Prince Henry's Room (8)**. Early in the seventeenth century the Council of the Duchy of Cornwall built a house at 17 Fleet Street. Used as a council chamber, it displays, in its very fine ceilings, the fleur-de-lis of the Prince of Wales and the initials PH, those of Prince Henry, James I's elder son, whose death before his father in 1612 left his younger brother to succeed to the throne as Charles I.

The gateway under the chamber leads into Inner Temple Lane and **Temple church (9).** Consecrated in 1185, this is one of only four remaining round churches in Britain. The long rectangular nave was added in the thirteenth century. It was after the disbandment of the Knights Templars in the fourteenth century that the 'men of law and their students' came to live here, and they have been here ever since. Above the wall seat in the round church there are some delightful stone carvings. Look for the devil whispering in a man's ear!

In **Crown Court Row (10)** it is recorded on a stone that Charles Lamb was born in a house here. The inscription reads:

Charles Lamb was born in the chambers which stood here
10th February 1775
' Cheerful Crown Office Row (place of my kindly engender)
..... a man would give something to have been born in such
places.'

Opposite Lamb's house are the gardens of the **Inner Temple (11)**. Here were plucked the roses – one white for York and one red for Lancaster – that marked the beginning of the Wars of the Roses in the fifteenth century. At the far end of the gardens is a fountain, a memorial to Charles Lamb, with another inscription that reads 'Lawyers were children once!'

For the curious or the literary explorer, Temple Gardens have many associations with Dickens. Fountain Court, with its fountain standing in the centre, reminds us that in *Martin Chuzzlewit* Ruth Pinch and her brother Tom met here, and Pump Court was where Tom Pinch acted as librarian; Mr Pip and his friend Herbert Pocket lived in Garden Court in *Great Expectations* while Paper Buildings has memories of Sir John Chester in *Barnaby Rudge* and the chambers of Mr Stryver KC in *A Tale of Two Cities*.

Middle Temple Hall (12) was built in 1574 and is one of the finest Tudor halls in England. The table is reputed to have been made from the wood of Sir Francis Drake's *Golden Hind*, but both the Middle Temple and Gray's Inn claim him as a member. The badge of the Middle Temple is the Agnus Dei (the Lamb with the nimbus and banner, with a red cross on a white background) and that of the Inner Temple is Pegasus (the winged horse); they can be seen on buildings around the Temple.

Walk up Middle Temple Lane and, passing through the doorway at the end, rejoin Fleet Street. Cross the roadway, where can be seen the site of **Temple Bar (13)** marked by a monument showing Queen Victoria and various bas-reliefs, including one of Sir Christopher Wren's Temple Bar. While never a fortified entrance to the City of London, Temple Bar marks the limits of the City's jurisdiction. When the monarch visits the City, he or she is stopped here by City officials. The Sword of State is offered to the monarch, who returns it as a sign that he or she comes in peace. Prior to its removal in the nineteenth century, Wren's gatehouse was used by the nearby Child's Bank as a depository for its archives, while in the days of decapitation heads were frequently displayed on the roof. One man used to make his living by hiring spy-glasses, at a farthing a time, so that the curious could obtain a better view of the skulls.

Walk away from Temple Bar. On the right are the **Royal Courts of Justice (14)**, popularly known as the Law Courts, designed by George Edmund Street and opened in 1882 by Queen Victoria. The Law Courts stand on land once owned by the Knights Templar, a military order of monks founded to protect the holy places of Palestine; their tilting yard was here.

Over the main entrance to the courts are three statues: to the left is Solomon, holding his temple, the only perfect building ever erected (in deference to which many architects, Street included, never allowed their buildings to be absolutely completed, and there is one partly carved column in the courts to bear witness to this); the statue on the right is King Alfred the Great, lawgiver to the English nation; and on the apex of the Great Hall's roof is Christ, His hand raised in blessing. This is the only secular building in London to be thus blessed. At the other end of the hall, in Carey Street, stands Moses with the Tablets of the Word – the Ten Commandments of the Old Testament. Each October at the Law Courts the City of London presents two faggots cut with a billhook and six horseshoes with sixty one nails to the Queen's Remembrancer. The faggots represent rent for The Moors in Shropshire and the horseshoes and nails rent for the forge in the parish of St Clement's. The same nails and shoes have been offered for five hundred years! Furthermore, nobody is quite sure where The Moors is, or whether the forge existed at all. There was until 1932, however, a smithy owned by W. H. Smith's, the booksellers, in a nearby street called Tweezers Alley.

Standing on an island in the middle of the Strand is the Central Church of the Royal Air Force, dedicated to **St Clement Danes (15),** built by Sir Christopher Wren in 1680, and restored after its damage by fire in the Second World War. St Clement was martyred, in about AD 100, by being attached to the anchor of a ship and thrown overboard; his sign, an anchor, can be seen on a number of buildings around the former parish. The floor of the nave of the church is paved with inscribed slates depicting Royal Air Force crests.

Follow the road round the Aldwych to Houghton Street. Turn right and walk past the London School of Economics to **Clare Market (16)**. The market was on land originally owned by the Earl of Clare and clients included the actors and actresses of Drury Lane. It developed into a 'rookery' – a place where criminals set themselves up to form a commune – and was later the site of the St Clement Danes parish workhouse.

The last stocks used in London were in **Portugal Street (17)**;

they were last used in 1826.

In Portsmouth Street is the **Old Curiosity Shop (18)**. Of all the tourist attractions in London this is the one with the most controversial past. There seems little doubt that Charles Dickens knew this shop when it was on its original site where the statue of Sir Henry Irving is today at the back of the National Portrait Gallery. Robert Allbut wrote in his book *London and Country Rambles with Charles Dickens*, published in 1895:

'The Old Curiosity Shop. A lady, personally acquainted with the great novelist, has informed the author that she was once taken by Mr Dickens to No.10, Green Street (approaching Leicester Square from the east) at the corner of Green and Castle Streets, behind the National Gallery, the business of curiosity dealing being then and there carried on. Mr Dickens himself localised this house as the home of Little Nell, pointing out an inner room – divided from the shop by a glass partition – as her bedroom. The premises are being now rebuilt.'

Those words were written after the Metropolitan Street Alterations Act of 1894, when the area around Charing Cross Road was being redeveloped. It seems highly likely that the shop was taken down and rebuilt in Portsmouth Street. Dickens died in 1870 and there is no mention of his having seen the shop on his way to Lincoln's Inn Fields, where he regularly gave public readings of extracts from his books.

When the architect Inigo Jones laid out **Lincoln's Inn Fields (19)** in 1618 he designed a number of houses surrounding them; numbers 59 and 60 remain as examples of his work, and Charles Dickens came next door to number 58 to read *The Chimes* to some of his more intimate friends, prior to publication.

In 1812-14 Sir John Soane, architect of the Bank of England, built three houses in Lincoln's Inn Fields, numbers 12 to 14. He set up house in number 13 and let the houses on either side. In his own house he gathered around himself and his family many items of architectural and artistic interest. Soane's disappointment that his sons did not follow him into the architectural profession led him to obtain an Act of Parliament to protect his collection, and the setting up of **Soane's Museum (20).** A visit to the museum will reveal, apart from the furnishings, a number of items of unusual interest: the face mask of Sarah Siddons, the famous eighteenth-century actress; arches from the old Palace of Westminster; the marble sarcophagus of Seti I which Soane brought from Egypt. He hoped to sell this to the British Museum but he failed and so retained it for his own collection. One of the surprises is the Picture Room, measuring some 10 feet (3 metres)

Part of the extraordinary collection in Soane's Museum.

square, which houses dozens of pictures hung on walls which open and close like cupboards. There are many of Soane's own drawings of commissioned work and competition entries, but perhaps the most important pictures in the room are those by William Hogarth of *The Rake's Progress* and *The Election*. Both series show life in the eighteenth century and are some of the finest satirical pictures of the Age of Reason. For serious architectural students the collection of drawings by the architects George Dance, Robert Adam and John Soane himself will be of special interest.

Since the nineteenth century Lincoln's Inn Fields has been an open space of some 12 acres (5 hectares). It has been a popular place for duels and in the centre of the Fields Lord William Russell was executed in 1683 for his part in the Rye House Plot. This was a conspiracy to murder Charles II and his brother James on their return from Newmarket at Rye House, near Hoddesdon, in Hertfordshire. A brass **plaque (21)** under the shelter in the middle records the execution.

Leave the Fields by Serle Street. At the junction with Carey Street there is a statue of **Sir Thomas More (22)**, commemorating his connection with Lincoln's Inn. More was born in Milk Street in the City and was admitted to Lincoln's Inn in 1496, after which he became a Member of Parliament. He opposed Henry VII's demand for money and, as a consequence, had to withdraw from public life. He came to the notice of Henry VIII and, after Cardinal Wolsey's fall from power, was appointed Lord Chancellor. Because of his strong religious beliefs he would not assist Henry VIII in obtaining his divorce from Catherine of Aragon, and for refusing to accept the Oath of Supremacy he was committed to the Tower of London. Found guilty on these charges and of treason he was executed on 6th July 1535. He was canonised by the Roman Catholic Church in 1935.

In Carey Street there are two **stones (23)** which mark the boundary of the two local parishes of St Clement Danes in the Strand, and St Dunstan-in-the-West, Fleet Street. The former has an anchor ring, and the latter the initials SDW reading anti-clockwise.

To the side of the boundary stones is a shop, first established in the seventeenth century, where ladies could purchase silver mouse-traps. In those days it was fashionable to powder the hair with flour, so it is hardly surprising that mice were attracted to it. Therefore, when going to bed at night, silver mouse-traps were placed on a convenient side table.

A few yards from the shop there is a gatehouse that leads into Lincoln's Inn New Square. Enter the square, but note that this entrance is closed every evening and all day Saturday and Sunday. It must be remembered that all Inns of Court are private property and must be treated as such by any visitors to them. At the far end of the square, on the right-hand side, is **Lincoln's Inn Chapel (24)**, designed by Inigo Jones in the seventeenth century. It replaced a medieval chapel which had become too small to serve the members of the Inn. The chapel is normally open from late morning to early afternoon Monday to Friday, with a public service on Sunday morning. A unique feature of the building is the open undercroft where 'men of law and their students might converse in inclement weather!' It has also been used for burials, and a framed plan showing the position of burials hangs on the wall.

Leave the Inn by the Chancery Lane gatehouse on the opposite side of the square from the chapel. On entering Chancery Lane, turn left. At number 53 Chancery Lane is the Aladdin's cave of London – the **London Silver Vaults (25)**. Here you may come just to view or to buy all kinds of silverware, old and new, from a complete canteen of cutlery to a silver tea service.

On leaving the vaults, it is a short walk back to Chancery Lane underground station.

Enclosed by a City wall

7
Enclosed by a City wall

The history of London's City wall begins in the second century AD, although the experts cannot agree as to exactly when it was built. One school of thought dates the wall from about AD 140, while another puts its building as late as AD190. It was certainly not built in AD 60-1 when Queen Boudicca razed Londinium (the Roman name for the City) to the ground, as a reprisal against the Romans who had assaulted her daughters and confiscated her lands on the death of her husband Prasutagus, king of the Iceni tribe.

When completed, the wall enclosed some 330 acres (133.5 hectares) of land and made London the fifth largest city in the Roman Empire. It is obvious from the different bondings used in the various sections which remain that a number of building gangs were used in the erection of the wall. As London had no quarries of its own, the materials used had to be brought in from outside: 'squared-off' Kentish ragstone formed the inner and outer faces of the wall while concrete and rubble filled in the centre. Every few feet of height (and this is the main evidence of different building gangs) one, two or three rows of Roman tiles were used as a bond before proceeding with the next 3 or 4 feet (0.9 to 1.2 metres) of wall. The finished structure stood about 30 feet (10 metres) high and running along the inside was a sentry walk, for the soldiers on guard duty. At a later date semicircular bastions were added, mainly on the eastern side of the City, the side most prone to attack from invaders or pirates approaching London from down-river. A number of these towers can still be seen along various stretches of the wall, in particular the corner bastion of the Cripplegate fort.

The main entrances to the City were Aldgate, Aldersgate, Newgate, Ludgate and Bridge or South Gate. The final stretch of the wall to be built stretched from the Blackfriars of today to the Wardrobe Tower of the Tower of London. Originally, it was thought that the river was sufficient defence in itself. Consequently the wall between these two points was the last built. Ironically it was the first to collapse – the river undermined the foundations and it fell into the river. A number of the buildings in Upper and Lower Thames Streets today have Roman wall as their foundation.

To cover the entire length of the completed wall one has to walk over 3 miles (5 km), but there are so many interesting places to visit on the way that the distance soon passes.

To many visitors to the **Tower of London (1)** the ruins at the south-east corner of the White Tower are merely something to hurry past on the way out, but to others they are the beginning of London Wall. They formed part of a bastion on the corner of the wall and were later adapted to form part of the Wardrobe Tower of the king's royal palace at the Tower. Examination of the remains showed Roman and later work in their construction.

Travellers arriving at **Tower Hill station (2)** to visit the Tower of London can find remains of the wall close to the station's entrances. Here can be seen a fine stretch of the Roman and the later wall of the City. Close by is one of London's earliest inscribed wall monuments, which commemorates the Procurator of Britain, the financial officer, between AD 61 and 65. It records the burial of 'Caius Iulius Alpinus Classicianus of the Fabian Tribe ... procurator of the Province of Britain...Iulius Pacata daughter of ...Indus his sorrowing wife.' Unfortunately only the top and the bottom portions of the stone have yet been found. The missing section probably recorded his long and distinguished career in the

The Roman Emperor Trajan stands by London's wall.

service of the Emperor Nero. Research has revealed that Classicianus was almost certainly the successor of Decianus Catus, whose actions were responsible for the uprising by Queen Boudicca. The original inscription is now in the British Museum collection in Great Russell Street. At the entrance to the open space in front of the wall stands an eighteenth-century Italian statue of the Emperor Trajan. It was found in a Southampton scrap merchant's yard by the Reverend 'Tubby' Clayton, of All Hallows by the Tower, and bought by the Tower Hill Improvement Trust. The Trust placed it here in 1980 when the area was being landscaped.

On the other side of the underground station are Coopers Row and **Wakefield House (3),** the former home of the interdenominational organisation founded by 'Tubby' Clayton in the First World War and called Toc H. The organisation takes its name from Talbot House – Toc H in signallers' language – and was started on the Flanders battlefields, 6 miles (10 km) from Ypres. Coopers Row is shown on early maps of the City as being Woodruffe Lane from the surname of the owner of the land, in turn derived from an English woodland flower that perhaps grows on the banks of the City walls. It retained its original title until 1750, when the coopers (barrel makers) were prominent in this area. Behind the office block on the right-hand side of the street is another fine stretch of the City wall. Here can be seen the construction of the Roman and the medieval wall, with the remains of a stairway and later windows. It is an excellent example of the wall at its prime. Passing through a modern postern gateway, one sees the formidable 30 feet (10 metres) which formed the outer side. A diagram on the side wall shows the route of the wall and the position of the bastions – rounded towers that were added later to strengthen the defence of the City. These towers enabled defenders to survey the area outside the walls without being exposed to attack.

In Jewry Street stands the former **Sir John Cass College (4),** now part of the City Guildhall University. It was founded in 1710 as the Sir John Cass Foundation and was for many years the only place in the City for advanced scientific study. On the wall are several plaques denoting ownership by the City of London – see the coat of arms of the City; other plaques are the parish boundary marks of St Botolph, Aldgate, while another, with a wheel on it, shows the boundary of St Katharine Cree, and lastly there is the Ward of Aldgate sign. As the name implies, Jewry Street was once one of the Jewish areas in London .

At the road junction where Leadenhall Street and Fenchurch Street join Aldgate stands the **Aldgate Pump (5)**. Before the piping of water into the City there was a series of pumps and conduits from which the water could be drawn. The present pump is a few yards from where its predecessor stood and as water from this pump had a different taste from the other local pumps efforts were made to trace the source. It was discovered that during its journey underground from the hills of Hampstead and Highgate it passed through a cemetery. Calcium from the bones gave its unique taste!

The 'Old Gate' (Aldgate) stood at the junction of Aldgate and Houndsditch where there is now a road island. A Corporation 'blue plaque' on a nearby building records its demolition in 1760. As its name implies, this gateway was one of the earliest to be built, leading as it did to the Roman road to East Anglia, via Colchester. It was rebuilt early in the twelfth century by the prior of the nearby Priory of the Holy Trinity. A document, bearing the date 1374, in the Guildhall Library records that Geoffrey Chaucer was granted a lease of the gate's chambers 'for the whole life of him the said Geoffrey'. At that time he was the Comptroller of the Wool Subsidy of the City, a post that he lost in 1386. While living here he wrote *The Legend of Good Women*, *The House of Fame* and *Troylus and Cryseyde*. Shortly after leaving the gate Chaucer set about writing his masterpiece *The Canterbury Tales*, perhaps inspired by the throng of people who daily passed under his rooms in the gate and whom he had seen from his window.

Between Aldgate and Bishopsgate the ditch which ran along the outside of the wall became known as Houndsditch from the number of dead dogs left there to rot. Today it is a busy street.

One of the largest monastic establishments of pre-Reformation London was Holy Trinity, Aldgate, which belonged to the Order of Augustinian Canons. Only an arch or two remain; they can be seen in the new office block at the junction of Mitre Street and Leadenhall Street. But **Mitre Square (6),** off Mitre Street, is on the site of the cloisters of the priory. It is also the site of one of the last known murders of the notorious Jack the Ripper.

The **Spanish and Portuguese Synagogue (7)** in Bevis Marks was first built in 1701. The architect was Mr Avis, a Quaker, who returned his fees to the synagogue as a gesture of goodwill. Queen Anne gave timber taken from the hulk of one of Her Majesty's ships. The building is a copy of the Portuguese Synagogue in Amsterdam, Holland, and has seven brass chandeliers made in Amsterdam. A pair of scroll mounts date from the late seventeenth century. The street in which the synagogue is situated – Bevis Marks – derives its name from the abbots of Bury St Edmunds, who had a house here prior to the Dissolution of the Monasteries in the sixteenth century.

Bishopsgate (8) commemorates the renowned Saxon Bishop of London, St Erkenwald, who had the original gateway built some time before his death in AD 693. The saintly prelate used to exact a toll of one piece of wood from all the carts loaded with wood coming into the City by way of the gate. Later, in the reign of Henry III, the maintenance of the gate became the responsibility of the Hanseatic merchants and in return they were allowed certain privileges within the City; however, until 1318 the Bishop was still responsible for the upkeep of the hinges. The gate, which the Hanseatic merchants rebuilt in 1471, lasted until the eighteenth century, when it shared the fate of the other seven gates and was demolished and sold as scrap. Drawings from the latter time show the upper storeys to be windowless and so uninhabitable. The building on the site of the gate has a stone mitre, a bishop's triangular-shaped hat, on it.

The church of **All Hallows, London Wall (9)**, is built at the side of and over the City wall.

Founded in 1333, incorporated in 1477, the **Worshipful Company of Carpenters (10)** first built a hall here in 1428. A land mine in May 1941 wrecked the hall and an explosion from gas mains in nearby London Wall completed the destruction. The company's records, charters, ordinances and furniture were saved, as was the Master's Garland, but the hall had to be rebuilt. The keystones of the arches at street level all portray famous architects and include William of Wykeham, Wren, Soane, Inigo Jones and Vanbrugh.

In 1246 a priory was set up outside the City wall and 'divided from Moorfields by a deep ditch'. By 1402 it had become a hospital for lunatics who, according to John Stow, were transferred from a hospice at Charing Cross as the king did not like it so near his palace. In 1675 the asylum was rebuilt in **Moorfields (11)**, now Moorgate, and was designed by Robert Hooke, with a lease of 999 years from the Corporation of London and an annual rent, if demanded, of one shilling (5p). Payment of the rent has never been requested! It stood 40 feet (12 metres) high and 540 feet (164 metres) long and was surrounded by a high wall.

Moorgate (12) was a major gateway into the City and dates from 1415 when Thomas Falconer, Lord Mayor of London, had the original gate built. It replaced a postern or pedestrian gateway. The area *outside* the wall, Moorfields, was used in the middle ages for recreational purposes. The river Walbrook started its journey through the City from the fields and in winter overflowed and froze, making London's first open-air ice rink. Apprentices tied the bones of animals to the soles of their shoes and used them as skates.

On the wall of **Moor House (13)** is a Corporation blue plaque commemorating Sir Ebenezer Howard, who founded the Garden City movement in 1899. Using the upper walkway between Moorgate and Cripplegate one sees the redevelopment of London Wall after the devastation of the Blitz of 1940-1, a development that continues today with new buildings replacing those built in the immediate post-war period.

In the fourteenth century Sir John Elsing founded **Elsing Priory (14)** for one hundred blind men. At the Dissolution of the Monasteries in the sixteenth century all the inhabitants were turned out and the buildings sold; the domestic buildings were used as a house until a fire later in the same century destroyed them. Owing to the bad state of repair of the church of **St Alphege, London Wall (15)**, the congregation moved into the chapel of the priory. All that

Exposed Roman wall alongside water gardens at Cripplegate.

ON THIS SITE AT 12·15 A·M
ON THE 25TH AUGUST 1940
FELL THE FIRST BOMB ON
THE CITY OF LONDON IN
THE SECOND WORLD WAR

The bomb memorial in Fore Street.

remains of the chapel today is the central crossing.

Nestling down among the buildings of modern London is a magnificent stretch of wall. By descending the stairs beside it one comes into a pleasant oasis and also gets an impression of the height and formidable approach of the wall to anyone attempting to scale it. Standing here, in what would have been the City ditch, it is easy to see how impenetrable the wall was in the middle ages. The lower portion is the *upper* part of the Roman wall, with the medieval walling on top capped by Tudor brickwork. The wall was kept in good order even after gunpowder made such defences superfluous and was used by the citizens as a means of getting about the City; it was preferable to use the wall as a bypass than to risk health and safety by walking through the narrow, often stinking, streets and alleys.

Bestriding London Wall at Cripplegate is **Roman House (16)**, on the Fore Street side of which can be seen an inscribed stone commemorating the first explosive bomb of the Second World War to fall on the City.

Cripplegate (17) was once a gate into the military compound or fort of London, but it was later enlarged to become a City gate. The name is derived from *crepel,* an Anglo-Saxon word for den or underground passage. Once the City gates were closed for the night, after the curfew bells had been rung, it was impossible to get into the City through any of the gateways but here, at Cripplegate, was an underpass which enabled persons able to prove their identity to enter.

In the churchyard of **St Giles, Cripplegate (18)**, stands a corner bastion of the Roman fort, and of the City wall. Excavation and rebuilding in the area of Cripplegate brought to light the guard

65

room of the **Roman fort (19).** It is possible to visit these ruins by enquiring at the reception desk of the nearby Museum of London.

Following excavations after the bombing of the Second World War a stretch of wall was uncovered in **Noble Street (20).** The results were to establish the line of the wall and lead to the discovery of the Roman fort. At the Gresham Street end of the site can be seen the foundations of the City wall, disappearing under the churchyard of St Anne and St Agnes, and the wall of the fort. Note particularly the remains of the guard tower which formerly stood on the corner of the fort.

When the City wall was first built, **Aldersgate (21)** became the north gate and as such became the 'Older-gate'. (An alternative derivation is that a man called Ealdred may have been responsible for its rebuilding at sometime.) A document of 1289 specifically mentions Aldersgate and it certainly would have been concerned with an order of 1282 which read: 'All the gates of the city are to be open by day: and at each gate there are to be two sergeants to open the same, skilful men, fluent of speech, who are to keep watch on persons coming and going so that no evil befall the City.' A later order, of the fourteenth century, says that each gate should have twelve men by day and twenty-four men by night, 'able-bodied, well instructed and well armed'. The gate was rebuilt in 1617 to the design of Gerald Christmas, the architect of nearby Northumberland House; its site is marked by a plaque. On the outer face of the gate was an equestrian statue of James I (VI of Scotland), who rode through its predecessor on coming to London to claim the throne of England. Until the Great Fire of London in 1666 the king's statue was flanked by the prophets Jeremiah and Samuel, but these were replaced in 1672 by a boy and girl. Judging by the picture on the churchyard wall in Little Britain, the gateway stood three storeys high and formed an impressive entrance into the City. At a later date it was used by a printer named John Daye who would waken his apprentices by calling out to them 'Awake for it is Daye!'. Among the books printed here was Foxe's *Book of Martyrs*, the first edition dating from 1563. Daye also published, in 1560, the *Church Music Book in England* and in 1570 the first English edition of Euclid. The records of the nearby parish church of St Botolph make interesting reading and shed light on another, social side of life at the gates. The churchwardens' accounts book for the year 1723 has an entry: 'Atte the Bull and Mouth about a woman big with child 1/- & gave the Watch at Aldersgate for getting her out of the parish 6d'.

Almost opposite the blue plaque which marks the site of Aldersgate (close by the Raglan public house) is another plaque marking the former site of the **Bull and Mouth Inn (22).** When the

Post Office bought the land here they demolished the inn. Today the building is used for commercial purposes rather than postal. The inn sign, a black bull with a large human mouth at its feet, can be seen in the nearby Museum of London.

Under the forecourt of the Post Office building in **Giltspur Street (23)** can be seen (after getting permission from the postal offices in King Edward Street) a corner bastion of the wall. Also on the nearby wall can be seen a blue plaque commemorating the site of the Giltspur Street compter. A compter was a small prison, often just a house where persons could be detained for a supposedly short period of time. Many compters were so overcrowded that often ten times the number they were designed to hold were housed in them.

Newgate (24), one of the oldest gateways into the City (traces of the Roman west gate of the City were found in 1874), has become synonymous with the prison that started in the rooms over the gate. Rebuilt after being damaged in the Great Fire, Newgate was first used as a prison in the eleventh century. The provision for the benefit of its inhabitants in the wills of wealthy persons in the middle ages was rated as a pious disposition. Much damage was

The Central Criminal Courts now occupy the site of Newgate prison.

done to the building during the Peasants' Revolt of 1381, which ended with the rebel leader, Wat Tyler, being stabbed to death by the Mayor of London, Sir William Walworth; the alleged weapon is now held by the Fishmongers' Company in their hall in Upper Thames Street. Money left for charitable purposes by Richard Whittington, four times Mayor of London, was used to repair the prison. After the 'No Popery Riots' of 1780 George Dance the Younger designed a new complex of buildings which, although larger than its predecessor, was often overcrowded. In 1831 the debtors' side of the prison, designed to hold one hundred, held 340 prisoners. A Select Commission on Prison Discipline of 1852 restricted its use as a prison to prisoners awaiting execution. In 1880 it ceased to be used as a prison, except during the sitting of the Central Criminal Courts, and was finally demolished early in the twentieth century. The last public execution, outside the debtors' doorway, was in May 1868, when Michael Barrett was hanged for his part in trying to blow up the Clerkenwell House of Detention, the remains of which are still under the Hugh Myddleton School in Clerkenwell. In recent years they have been open to the public, who are conducted round by well-versed guides.

The **Central Criminal Courts (25)** now stand on the site of the former Newgate Prison and 200 feet (61 metres) above street level stands the statue of Justice, without the usual blindfold, which is carefully cleaned twice a year. Over the main entrance to the Courts are sculptured figures of Truth, Justice and the Recording Angel, while the inscription reads 'Defend the children of the poor and punish the wrongdoer', taken from Psalm 72, selected by the Dean of Westminster and approved by the Archbishop of Canterbury. In the main foyer of the Central Criminal Courts is the only statue of a woman to be found within the precincts of an English court of justice. Based on a painting by Gibson and modelled by Alfred Drury RA, it is of Elizabeth Fry, the famous Quaker prison reformer born in Norwich in 1780, who died in 1845 and was buried in the former Friends' burial ground in Barking. (The building is now a Sikh temple but the burials were left undisturbed.)

In old English *ludgeat* means 'postern' or 'back doorway'. Whether **Ludgate (26)** was as old a gate as Newgate is open to dispute, but remains of a Roman cemetery have been found along the line of Fleet Street, which suggests that there was a road here in Roman times. The Romans did not, as a rule, bury within the precincts of a city, but almost invariably by the side of roads. King Lud, a mythical king of Britain, is said to have founded London, which is in fact 'Lud's Town', in days too far back in history to be recorded. A statue of King Lud and his sons taken from the gate can be seen at the church of **St Dunstan-in-the-West,** Fleet Street.

8
City churches: east of St Paul's Cathedral

The number of parishes in the City of London at the end of the middle ages has been conservatively estimated at between 120 and 130, of which some three dozen have survived as parish or guild churches. After the Great Fire of London in 1666 fifty-three churches were rebuilt by Sir Christopher Wren, and since the seventeenth century twenty-one have been pulled down, mainly to make way for office buildings. But still today some think that there are too many churches within the 'one square mile', with its now vastly reduced resident population

Of the original 120, seven medieval churches remain in the City. They are: All Hallows by the Tower (interior rebuilt after the Second World War); St Olave, Hart Street; St Helen, Bishopsgate (this has now been reordered after being severely damaged by IRA bomb explosions in 1992 and 1993); St Giles, Cripplegate; St Sepulchre without Newgate; St Andrew Undershaft (also a victim of bomb explosions in the 1990s); and St Bartholomew the Great, Smithfield. St Ethelburga, Bishopsgate, was reduced to a shell in the IRA bombings and its future has yet to be settled.

Add to the above the thirty-five churches which were not rebuilt by Wren after the Great Fire, including St Botolph, Aldersgate, St Botolph, Bishopsgate, and St Botolph, Aldgate, which with All Hallows, London Wall, form an arc around the perimeter of the City. For good measure add the church of St Katherine Cree, built in 1628-31, which also escaped the Fire, and you can then complete your survey of the non-Wren churches of the City by including St Mary Woolnoth by Nicholas Hawksmoor.

Under the City of London (Guild Churches) Act of 1952 and the City Scheme of 1954, the City of London was divided into twenty-three parishes and fifteen guild churches. The latter have no parochial functions and do not hold Sunday services but have been allotted special functions within the Church of England, e.g. St Ethelburga, Bishopsgate, was, until it was declared redundant in 1990, responsible for the Church's healing ministry.

This and the following two chapters describe many of the parish and guild churches of interest to the seeker of the unusual.

The nearest convenient underground station for this tour is Aldgate, served by the Circle Line.

From the station turn right and it is a short walk to the parish church of **St Botolph, Aldgate (1)**, one of the three City churches dedicated to Botolph, the saint after whom the town of Boston,

Lincolnshire, is named. The church was rebuilt in the 1740s by George Dance and has a ceiling designed in 1889 by John Francis Bentley, the architect of Westminster's Roman Catholic cathedral. When, in 1554, the Earl of Suffolk, Lady Jane Grey's father, was beheaded on Tower Hill his head was placed, as was the custom at that time, on the roof of a City gate. The earl's head was displayed on Aldgate. It was later removed and buried in the forecourt of the church, from which it has now disappeared!

Continue down Aldgate and fork right into Leadenhall Street. The guild church of **St Katherine Cree (2)** stands on the corner of Cree Lane and Leadenhall Street. At the dissolution of the Holy Trinity Priory (also called Christ Church), Aldgate, Henry VIII offered the local people the great priory church for worship, but they preferred the small church or chapel that stood on the corner of the monastic burial ground. It was dedicated to St Katherine. The curious suffix 'Cree' is a reminder of its original situation, Cree being synonymous with Christ Church.

Buried by the high altar is Sir John Gayer, Lord Mayor of London in 1646, who while on an expedition across an eastern desert became separated from his party and met a lion! He immediately fell on his knees and started praying, and when he opened his eyes the lion had moved away! In gratitude, he left money for a sermon to be preached on every anniversary. Although the money has now been absorbed into the general funds of the Parochial

John Stow's memorial in St Andrew Undershaft.

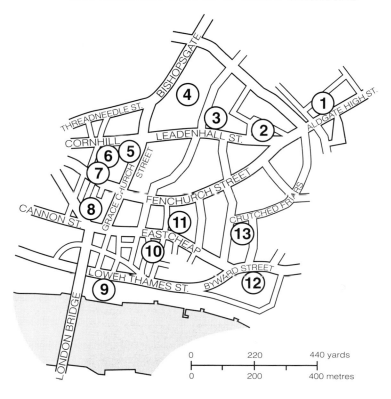

City churches: east of St Paul's Cathedral

1. St Botolph, Aldgate
2. St Katherine Cree
3. St Andrew Undershaft
4. St Helen, Bishopsgate
5. St Peter upon Cornhill
6. St Michael, Cornhill
7. St Edmund, King and Martyr
8. St Clement, Eastcheap
9. St Magnus the Martyr
10. St Mary-at-Hill
11. St Margaret Pattens
12. All Hallows by the Tower
13. St Olave, Hart Street

Charities of 1871, the sermon is still given at the Lion Service on 16th October each year. In the south-west corner seek out the head (capital) belonging to a former church; if this is still in its original position, then the present church must be built on top!

A short distance away from St Katherine's, on the corner of St Mary Axe, is the parish church of **St Andrew Undershaft (3).** One of the maypoles of the City was regularly erected in Leadenhall Street outside this church, on May Day, to honour the Blessed Virgin Mary at the start of the month dedicated to her. After use the pole was taken down and strapped to the outside wall of the church – hence the suffix 'Undershaft'. One of the most eminent Londoners, John Stow, whose famous book *A Survay* (sic) *of London* was first published in 1598, lies buried in the church, having died in 1605. His book was the first guide and history of the City of London and is still looked upon as being a reference book for historians and scholars today. His tomb in the north-east corner of the church shows Stow seated at his desk writing.

Cross the open paved area opposite St Andrew's to reach **St Helen's church (4),** in a secluded courtyard off Bishopsgate, surrounded by tall office buildings. This was built as a dual church; one half of the building was used by Benedictine nuns, and the other by the parish, with a wall between the two. At the time of the Dissolution of the Monasteries in the sixteenth century the dividing wall was removed to make the largest parish church in the City. Dedicated to St Helen, the mother of the Emperor Constantine and discoverer of the True Cross, this is one of the real gems among the City's churches. In the north wall can be seen the squint or hagioscope through which the nuns in the infirmary beyond could see the altar. Over the nuns' squint is the only Easter sepulchre left in the City, used to 'bury' the consecrated Host of the Mass on Maundy Thursday until, after due watch had been kept, it was resurrected on Easter Day. In the eastern portion of this side of the church there are two tombs of interest: one is that of Sir Thomas Gresham, founder of the Royal Exchange, the other of Sir Julius Caesar. Also buried in the church, though his tomb is no longer above ground, was Francis Bancroft, 'an officer of the Corporation', who was the founder of the Bancroft Charity and School (now at Woodford).

On the highest point of the City stands the church of **St Peter upon Cornhill (5)**; some would have it that it is on the site of the oldest church in London. The story is that King Lucius, himself a legendary figure, founded it as the principal church of his kingdom. This church is one of only two, the other being St Margaret Lothbury, to possess a post-Great Fire rood-screen. Originally these screens would have had the crucifixion scene on them to remind the faithful of Christ's death; today they simply divide the choir from the congregation. Nearly all the woodwork of this church is original seventeenth-century and can easily be identified by its colour – blood red or brown. Wren gave instructions that all wood should be dipped in animals' blood in Smithfield Market before being stained. The blood has acted as a preservative and none of the original panelling has either woodworm or dry rot! In the vestry can be seen a brass plaque commemorating the early foundation of the parish, and the original Father Smith keyboard on which Mendelssohn played in September 1840. However, the largest object in the room is a withdrawing table, which is unique. Used in the church for communion services, it was removed – withdrawn – after use, thereby emphasising the Protestant faith's belief that the service is not a sacrifice on an altar. Outside the vestry, high on the wall, are the former bread shelves.

On the building to the right of the main entrance of the church, in Cornhill, can be seen the 'unholy trinity', three devils. Placed there by an architect who lost a dispute with the rector and churchwardens, they record his personal feelings towards the people of the church.

A few yards further down Cornhill is the parish church of **St**

The phoenix pew end in St Michael Cornhill.

Michael, Cornhill (6). When Wren designed a new church for the parish after the Great Fire he was given clear instructions that it should be in the Gothic (medieval) style. Consequently he did not raze the previous building to the ground but incorporated as much as he could into his church. Doubtless he would have preferred to build in the new Renaissance form! In Saxon times the church was given to the Abbey of Evesham in Worcestershire, which maintained connections with the parish until the Dissolution of the Monasteries. The tower is a facsimile of the chapel tower of Magdalen College, Oxford, and was the work of Nicholas Hawksmoor, a protégé and successor of Wren. Somewhere in the former churchyard, now laid out as a garden, lie buried the father and grandfather of John Stow, the sixteenth-century historian and writer. The carved pew ends are worth noting: look out for the one with St Michael the Archangel killing Satan, and another one depicting the phoenix.

Take the alley by the side of St Michael's to reach George Court. Sir Christopher Wren's design for the spire of **St Edmund, King and Martyr (7)**, in Lombard Street, is shaped like a lighthouse, a reminder that after the Great Fire the nearby parish of St Nicholas Acons was merged with St Edmund's, Nicholas being the patron saint of seamen as well as of children. This church was the only one damaged by bombing in the City during the *First* World War. High up on the west wall there is a brass memorial plaque to Charles Melville Hays, President of the Grand Trunk Railway, who was drowned when the SS *Titanic* sank in 1912 on her maiden voyage after colliding with an iceberg.

Opposite St Edmund is St Clement's Lane, at the end of which is the parish church of **St Clement, Eastcheap (8),** whose claim to be the original 'Oranges and Lemons' church of the nursery rhyme is based on the fact that these fruits were once unloaded and sold within the boundaries of the parish. The church has some bread shelves, from which bread for the poor was taken after the main Sunday service. A number of churches of the City had money left to them from which they bought loaves of bread for charitable distribution. In most instances today the moneys have either run out or have been incorporated into other charitable funds.

At the end of St Clement's Lane turn left into King William Street and walk towards London Bridge. **St Magnus the Martyr (9),** Lower Thames Street, was once at the foot of old London Bridge and is so described in early documents as *Ecclesia St Magni Civitatis London juxta pedem, vel as pedem Ponti London* – the church of St Magnus at the foot of London Bridge. Today the church is almost surrounded by office buildings and the only reminders of London Bridge are stones in the churchyard, from the medieval and nineteenth-century bridges. The church was one of the first to be destroyed in the Great Fire and was rebuilt by Wren ten years later. Safely locked away in a reliquary is a relic of the True Cross which every Good Friday is venerated by the faithful. Whether Miles Coverdale, translator of the first complete English Bible, would approve, is open to debate, as he preached against images and resigned his rectorship in 1563 for puritanical reasons. Originally buried in the church of St Bartholomew-by-the-Exchange (demolished in 1840), he was later transferred here.

Turn right out of St Magnus and cross Lower Thames Street by the footbridge. The entrance of **St-Mary-at-Hill (10)** is in Lovat Lane, which runs from Eastcheap down to Billingsgate. The church was only partly destroyed in the Great Fire and repaired by Wren. Later other portions of the church were replaced. In 1988 fire again severely damaged the church, which had to be gutted, leaving the interior without the superb wood carving for which the church was famous. In the west porch can be seen a Doom or Resurrection Stone depicting the Last Judgement with all the souls rising out of the tombs and being judged by St Michael the Archangel. Some are directed towards the heavenly city while others are dragged down into the jaws of Hell!

The door by the Doom will take you through passageways to Eastcheap and **St Margaret Pattens (11)**. Said by some to have obtained its strange suffix because pattens, a kind of shoe, were made in the parish, or because in medieval times a family called Patins were great benefactors of the church, today St Margaret Pattens provides an interesting oasis in the midst of an area full of offices. There are several unique features and items in the church.

The Doom carving in St Mary-at-Hill.

On the north side of the choir can be seen an ornately backed seat: this is the punishment seat, and here children who were misbehaving in church would be made to sit until the service was over. The beadle who brought the children to the chair had his own private pew behind it, and this too is worth examining for it is unique in the City. On the south wall of the church, in a glass-fronted cabinet, are samples of pattens, and buried nearby is James Donaldson, who was the City Garbler, an inspector of drugs in the seventeenth century. In the tower hangs a pre-Great Fire bell which can still be heard tolling over the City it has served so well. At the back of the church, standing on either side of the entrance doorway, is a set of raised pews on whose ceiling are the initials C W, said, according to one writer, to stand for Christopher Wren, this being his favourite church. They also stand for Church Warden!

The church better known today as **All Hallows by the Tower (12)** also boasts of being 'All Hallows Barking Church'; the latter title reminds us that this church was once owned by the Abbey Church of Barking, a convent set up by St Erkenwald, whose sister became the abbess. One of the few churches to survive the Great Fire, it was damaged in the Second World War, when a Saxon doorway and part of a cross were exposed. In the crypt under the church can be seen a model of Roman *Londinium*, remains of a Roman villa, monumental brasses and coffin plates. There is also a columbarium for the ashes of departed members of the Toc H Movement, whose mother church All Hallows is today. In the small chapel here the altar stone dates from the thirteenth century. Access to the crypt is allowed only when a member of staff is present. As the church is on the edge of Tower Hill a number of those executed there were buried in the church. The body of Archbishop Laud, who was executed in 1645, was later transferred to St John's College, Oxford.

From All Hallows turn left along Tower Street to Seething Lane on the right and follow to the end. 'Our own church' is how Samuel Pepys, the diarist, described **St Olave, Hart Street (13)**, and Charles Dickens renamed the church 'Saint Ghastly Grim' in his book *The Uncommercial Traveller*. What could be more natural than for both Samuel and his young wife Elizabeth to be buried 'near the Holy Table' in this church. Dickens's title for the church doubtless stemmed from the skulls and crossbones on the archway into the churchyard from Seething Lane. The church was another of those which survived the Great Fire but was badly damaged in the Second World War. The pulpit, by Grinling Gibbons, came from St Benet's, Gracechurch Street (which was demolished in 1867), and St Katherine Colman supplied the organ keyboard, whose white notes were black! At the Seething Lane entrance there is a notice board that includes the line 'Mother Goose was buried in the church 1586, 14th September'.

Skulls and bones decorate the entrance to the churchyard at St Olave, Hart Street.

9
City churches: City centre

The Bank underground station, on the Central and Northern lines, is an ideal place to start a walk around the churches that are in the City centre.

St Mary Woolnoth (1) is at the junction of Lombard Street and King William Street, a short walk away from the station, and was designed by Nicholas Hawksmoor in the early eighteenth century. Notice how the architect, by excluding all windows in the lower storeys, has turned the building into an almost sound-proof box. Edward Lloyd, in whose coffee-house in Tower Street Lloyd's of London was founded in 1689, was buried in the church in 1713, his coffee-house having moved to Lombard Street some time before. It was during the nineteenth-century restoration of the church by William Butterfield that the galleries were removed. Today all that is left of them is the panelling that has been attached to the side walls, making them look like drawers of a filing cabinet waiting to be opened. On the north side of the altar is a marble pyramidal tablet commemorating the rectorship of the Reverend John New-ton. It reads: 'To the memory of the Rev'd John Newton, once an infidel and libertine, a servant of slaves of Africa, 28 years rector of this church'. He was a buccaneer who 'saw the Light' during a violent storm at sea. According to tradition there was a church here in pre-Conquest times, and the suffix Woolnoth is the name of the founder.

A short walk along King William Street, on the right-hand side is Abchurch Lane. Here is to be found **St Mary Abchurch (2)**, where a medieval crypt has been found under the forecourt. A letter, found in 1946 and signed by Grinling Gibbons, confirms that he did much of the carving in this church. The dome is one of Sir Christopher Wren's finest achievements. Over 40 feet (12 metres) across, it is supported only by the brick walls. There are various theories as to how or why the lane and church were so named. One relates that the church stands on rising ground and so became known as Upchurch. Another source, Harben's *Dictionary of London*, says that Ab was all or part of a personal name. In the lane lived John Moore, whose celebrated worm-powder caused Alexander Pope to write:

> *O learned friend of Abchurch Lane*
> *Who sett'st our entrails free!*
> *Vain is thy art, thy powder vain*
> *Since worms shall eat e'en thee.*

St Stephen, Walbrook (3), nestles behind the Mansion House, the home of the Lord Mayor of London during his term of office. Standing originally by the side of the river Walbrook, the church was first mentioned in 1096 but at that time was on the other side of the river! Stow in his *Survay* records 'the fair church of St Stephen, lately built on the east side of Walbrook, for the old church stood on the west side, in place where now standeth the parsonage house, and therefore so much nearer the brook, even on its bank'. Legend records that whenever the builders tried to rebuild the church on its original site, every morning when they returned to work the stones had been removed across the river. Obviously the angels had decided where the new church should be built! In more recent years the church has become famous as the centre of the Samaritans movement that was founded here in 1953 by Prebendary Chad Varah. The movement's aim is to prevent suicidal tendencies and to give counselling to those people experiencing stress and problems in their lives. Chad Varah's original Mansion House 9000 telephone is on display. In 1986 a new altar was placed in the church. The work of the sculptor Henry Moore, it caused much

Henry Moore's altar in St Stephen, Walbrook.

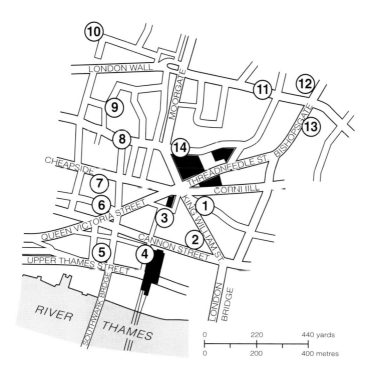

City churches: City centre

1. St Mary Woolnoth
2. St Mary Abchurch
3. St Stephen, Walbrook
4. St Michael Paternoster Royal
5. St James, Garlickhithe
6. St Mary Aldermary
7. St Mary-le-Bow
8. St Lawrence, Jewry
9. St Mary, Aldermanbury
10. St Giles, Cripplegate
11. All Hallows, London Wall
12. St Botolph, Bishopsgate
13. St Ethelburga, Bishopsgate
14. St Margaret, Lothbury

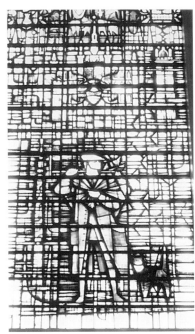

(Left) A modern representation of Dick Whittington and his cat in St Michael Paternoster Royal, and (right) St James, Garlickhithe, which was last restored after a crane fell upon it.

discussion at the time of its arrival.

On leaving the church turn left and walk down Walbrook to Dowgate Hill, at the end of which is College Street and the church of **St Michael Paternoster Royal (4).** The church's suffix reminds one that this is the Vintry Ward where, in the middle ages, wine was unloaded, particularly from La Reole near Bordeaux. The 'Paternoster' comes from a nearby Paternoster (Our Father) home where rosaries were made. This is Dick Whittington's church and in a modern stained glass window in the south wall can be seen the famous mayor of London and his cat. In a restoration of the church a mummified cat was found in the roof of the building – was it Dick Whittington's? Today as one of the guild churches of the City it serves as the headquarters of the work of the Mission to Seamen.

From Whittington's church turn right along College Street and across Queen Street to Skinners Lane and so to Garlick Hill and the parish church of **St James, Garlickhithe (5).** The original church was built in 1326 but destroyed in the Great Fire; rebuilt by Wren, it recently suffered damage when a crane working nearby collapsed on to the building. All has now been splendidly restored.

During a restoration in the nineteenth century a skeleton was found under the floor in the area of the choir. For nearly one hundred years nobody knew who it was. Was he some lost Lord Mayor of London or just another parishioner. Research carried out in 1995 revealed that he was a seventeen-year-old seaman named Seagrave Chamberlain to whom there is a memorial tablet on the north wall inside the church. The answer had been there for all to see, and nobody saw it ! His skeleton has been carefully cleaned and now he lies in his coffin in the bell chamber of the church. It is said that the choir boys used to dance around him when he was locked in a cupboard in the vestibule. Some visitors have even claimed to have seen his ghost!

From St James turn right up Garlick Hill and cross Queen Victoria Street. In former times there were as many as six churches within the walls of the City dedicated to the Blessed Virgin Mary, so each had to have its own suffix. In the case of **St Mary Aldermary (6)** in Queen Victoria Street the 'alder' means that it was the older, or elder, Mary (St Mary-le-Bow sometimes being described as St Mary Newchurch). The present church has restricted opening times. It was rebuilt by Wren after the Fire and displays the Gothic style of architecture so dearly loved by its former parishioners. Here, as at other medieval churches that Wren rebuilt, there was much left after the Fire and he saw fit to restore it to its former medieval glory. Note the fine reproduction fan-vaulting of the ceiling. On the south wall of the sanctuary area there hangs the White Ensign Association's flag, a reminder of its connections with the church.

Leave the church by the south door, turn right and walk along to Bow Lane, where at the far end is the parish church of **St Mary-le-Bow (7)**. Built on pre-Conquest arches ('bows'), it has an interior completely rebuilt since 1945. The Hanging Rood displays the Crucifixion of Christ with attendant figures of St Mary and St John and the additional figures of St Mary Magdalene and the Centurion. It was the gift of the Church of Germany as an act of reparation. Designed by John Hayward (who also designed the stained glass windows), it was carved by Otto Irsara of Oberammergau. The keystones of the arches depict King George VI as well as the architect of the restoration, Laurence King. The balcony over the entrance doorway to the church was put there by Wren and was intended to be used by kings and queens watching tournaments and processions in Cheapside, but it has never been used. Although Charles II was to have watched a procession from it, he heard rumours of a possible assassination plot and stayed at home! Children born within the sound of Bow bells are 'registered' Cockneys.

Cross over Cheapside and walk right along to King Street, at the end of which is the guild church of **St Lawrence, Jewry (8)**, standing within the shadow of the Guildhall, from where the City is governed. The curiously shaped weathervane shows the grid-iron, the symbol of the martyrdom of St Lawrence. He was mar-tyred in AD 258 by being burned alive on a gridiron, hence the sign. He is also the patron saint of the Worshipful Company of Girdlers, whose crest shows him on his gridiron. The beautiful modern glass window in the vestibule has the figure of Sir Christopher Wren flanked by his master carver (Grinling Gibbons) and master mason (Nicholas Stone), with small pictures of the modern rebuilding underneath.

As a memorial to Sir Winston Churchill, the former church of **St Mary, Aldermanbury (9),** was transferred bodily in 1966 to Westminster College, University of Fulton, Missouri, in the United States of America, where Sir Winston made his famous Iron Curtain speech in 1946. The phrase 'the Iron Curtain' denoted the barrier of secrecy created by the former USSR and her satellites along the Stettin-Trieste line, when all the states on the eastern side of the line were cut off from western Europe. The site of the church is now laid out as a garden and the medieval walls are exposed to view. During the excavations the site of the grave of 'bloody' Judge Jeffreys was rediscovered. He earned the epithet for the cruelty of the sentences he passed at the so-called 'Bloody As-sizes', when he presided at the trial of the followers of the Duke of Monmouth, defeated at the battle of Sedgemoor in 1685, many of whom he had whipped, transported or hanged. Standing in the former churchyard is the memorial to Heminge and Condell, pub-lishers of Shakespeare's plays in the early seventeenth century. The church's suffix refers to the house ('bury') of the Aldermen of the Common Council of the City of London which stood, and still stands, within the parish boundaries.

Standing alone in the Barbican is the parish church of **St Giles, Cripplegate (10),** another of the remaining pre-Fire churches of the City. The marriage of Oliver Cromwell to Elizabeth Bourchier took place here in 1620, and the burial of John Milton in 1647. There is a statue of Milton within.

Return to London Wall, turn to the left and walk along to the guild church **of All Hallows, London Wall (11).** The church had been for a number of years the headquarters of the Council for the Care of Churches but in 1993 the building was badly damaged in the 'Bishopsgate Bombing'. When it was a parish church before the Second World War, at services the preacher left his stall in the choir, entered the vestry built on an old bastion of the City wall, then walked up a short flight of steps, through a doorway into the

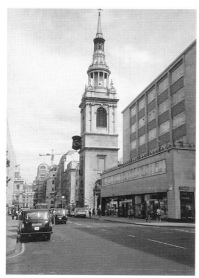

(Left) St Mary-le-Bow in Cheapside and (right) St Giles, Cripplegate, where John Milton was buried.

pulpit in the church. By so doing he had left London and returned to preach!

Continue along London Wall until Bishopsgate is reached and turn left to the parish church of **St Botolph, Bishopsgate (12),** rebuilt by James Gold between 1725 and 1729. It was first recorded in the thirteenth century. In the churchyard stands the former parish school with its figures of a boy and girl in their uniform.

Walk back down Bishopsgate, where on the left are the ruins of the former parish church of **St Ethelburga, Bishopsgate (13),** named after the first abbess of Barking, the daughter of Ethelbert, the Christian king of Kent. It was one of the finest of the smaller medieval churches of the City until it was blasted by the IRA bomb that exploded in Bishopsgate on 24th April 1993. The font, which dated from the middle ages, had a Greek palindrome inscription of the nineteenth century. Sir Ninian Comper was responsible for the screen and loft, pews, pulpit and panelling. Miraculously the wall painting by Hans Feibusch on the east wall survived the disaster. But the long-term future of the church has yet to be resolved.

Continue on, then turn right into Threadneedle Street. Turn right at the Bank of England up Bartholomew Lane to Lothbury. Behind the Bank of England is the parish church of **St Margaret, Lothbury (14).** The suffix comes either from the Lopa family who used to live here, or because it was a 'loathsome' place because of the proximity of the Founderers Company. At least three other churches designed by Wren have made their contribution to the beauty of this church. From All Hallows, Upper Thames Street, come the candelabra, the tester of the pulpit and the rood screen. This last is a match for that in St Peter, Cornhill, in its rarity value; it was a gift of Theodore and Jacob Jacobsen in 1689. St Olave, Jewry, provided the communion rail. The font, which is attributed to Grinling Gibbons, portrays the baptism of Christ by St John the Baptist, St Philip baptising the Ethiopian eunuch, the return of the dove to Noah on his Ark, and Adam and Eve in Paradise. Walking back alongside the Bank of England brings you to Bank underground station.

The font in St Margaret, Lothbury.

10
City churches: around St Paul's

From St Paul's underground station it is a short walk across the end of Cheapside to the parish church of **St Vedast, Foster Lane (1),** which now serves a combination of fourteen parishes. It is the only church in London to be dedicated to Vedast, who was bishop of Arras, in France, in the sixth century. Indeed there is record of only two other such dedications in England, one at Norwich, where only a street bears his name, and the other at Tathwell in Lincolnshire. During the restoration of the 1960s several items of furniture from other Wren churches were brought here: the font from St Anne and St Agnes; the pulpit from All Hallows, Bread Street (demolished 1878); the carved organ case from St Bartholomew-by-Exchange; while the reredos was designed for St Christopher-le-Stocks, which was pulled down in 1781 to make room for an extension to the Bank of England. The ceiling of the church is painted with silver, aluminium and gilt.

Turn right outside the church and walk along Foster Lane to the church of **St Anne and St Agnes (2)**. Early records list the church as being 'by-the-willows' so presumably there was a stream nearby. The dual dedication of St Anne (the grandmother of Christ) and St Agnes (a teenage girl beheaded in fourth-century Rome) is a curious one. The church is now used by the Lutheran Church.

Again take a right turn at the entrance to the churchyard and Gresham Street leads to Aldersgate and the parish church of **St Botolph, Aldersgate (3),** just outside the site of the gate into the City. It was rebuilt in the eighteenth century, possibly by Nathaniel Wright. The east window of eighteenth-century glass depicts the 'Agony in the Garden', the work of John Pearson from a painting by Nathaniel Clarkson. The memorial cloister in the churchyard, erected at the instigation of George Frederick Watts, the artist, commemorates everyday deeds of heroism. Watts is commemorated by a small bronze figure. The church, once declared redundant, is now a thriving one during the week.

Along the north side of the church is Little Britain. This ultimately leads to Smithfield and the priory church of **St Bartholomew the Great (4)**. Founded in 1123 by Rahere, a courtier of Henry I, the church served as an Augustinian priory until the Dissolution of the Monasteries in the sixteenth century. Today it is the parish church of the area, having been acquired by the parish at the Dissolution. Parts of the church and monastic buildings were sold, the parishioners retaining the old choir for their services. The last prior, Prior Bolton, built a watching window in the triforium opposite to the tomb of Rahere, and on the window can be seen his rebus, a punning stone depicting a crossbow 'bolt' piercing a 'tun' or large cask. In the south aisle can be seen the memorial to Edward Cooke, who died in 1652. The inscription reads:

> *Unsluce yor briny floods, what! can ye keepe*
> *Yor eyes from teares and see the marble weep,*
> *Burst out for shame: or if yee find noe vent*
> *or teares, yet stay, and see the stones relent.*

The stone of the tablet easily condenses water in damp weather, and the drops were said to be tears, that is until they placed a radiator underneath – then the 'tears' dried up!

Walk across the roadway from the priory church to the Hospital of St Bartholomew's, also founded by Rahere. Here on the left inside the gateway is **St Bartholomew the Less (5),** founded at the same time as the hospital to act as its parish church. Parts of the building date back to the middle ages, including a fifteenth-century monumental brass. Inigo Jones, the Palladian architect, was baptised in the predecessor of the present building. The church was

Prior Bolton's watching window in St Bartholomew the Great.

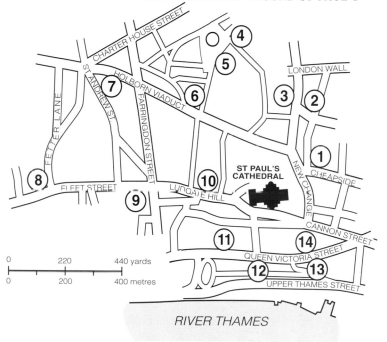

City churches: around St Paul's

1. St Vedast, Foster Lane
2. St Anne and St Agnes
3. St Botolph, Aldersgate
4. St Bartholomew the Great
5. St Bartholomew the Less
6. St Sepulchre without Newgate
7. St Andrew, Holborn
8. St Dunstan-in-the-West
9. St Bride, Fleet Street
10. St Martin within Ludgate
11. St Andrew by the Wardrobe
12. St Benet, Paul's Wharf
13. St Mary Somerset
14. St Nicholas Cole Abbey

rebuilt in 1789 under the direction of George Dance the Younger, who retained the medieval tower, vestry and west wall. The church was rebuilt again in 1823, this time by Thomas Hardwick, who kept the unusual octagonal plan and shape of the previous building.

Leave the hospital by way of the main gateway, turn left and walk down Giltspur Street, where, on the corner, is the present church of **St Sepulchre without Newgate (6).** It stands on the site of a Saxon church and was rebuilt in 1440 by Sir John Popham. Although only damaged at the time of the Great Fire, it was repaired by Wren. The exterior of the church shows many of the architectural features associated with the Gothic (medieval) form, including the windows reinstated in the nineteenth century, while the interior is all that one would expect of Wren and the Renaissance. Being in close proximity to the Old Bailey, the Central Criminal Court, which stands on the site of the Newgate prison opposite, the church has many stories connected with them. Robert Dowe, a merchant tailor by trade, left a bequest of fifty pounds in his will in order that, on the eve of execution, a priest might exhort those about to die to repent:

All you that in the condemned hole do lie,
Prepare you, for tomorrow you shall die.
Watch all, and pray; the hour is drawing near
That you before the Almighty must appear.
Examine well yourselves, in time repent,
That you may not to eternal flames be sent,
And when St Sepulchre's bell in the morning tolls
The Lord have mercy on your souls.
Past twelve o'clock.

The bequest has now been appropriated by the Charity Commissioners for the benefit of deserving prisoners on their discharge. John Wesley, in his *Journal* for 13th October 1784, noted after visiting the prisoners: 'When the bellman came at twelve o'clock to tell them (as usual) "Remember you are to die today", they cried out, "Welcome news, welcome news".'

With St Sepulchre on your right, continue to the further end of

The Resurrection Stone outside St Andrew, Holborn.

the Holborn Viaduct and the guild church of **St Andrew, Holborn (7)**. This is the administrative centre for the Archdeaconry of Hackney. The church now houses the mortal remains of Thomas Coram, who began the Foundling Hospital for deserted children in Hatton Garden in 1741; it was later moved to a new site in Lamb's Conduit Fields. The font, pulpit and organ all come from the chapel of the Foundling Hospital. On the outside north wall is a Resurrection Stone showing the world on Doomsday when all the dead rise out of their graves and, after their souls have been duly weighed by St Michael the Archangel, are allowed into Heaven or taken down into Hell. Most of the figures are completely naked, but bishops and popes come out of their coffins wearing their mitres and crowns.

To visit **St Dunstan-in-the-West (8)** from Holborn cross over Holborn Circus and walk down New Fetter Lane to Fleet Street, where turn right. The church is a short distance from the junction of the two roadways. The present church of St Dunstan dates from 1832, when it was rebuilt by John Shaw, following the widening of Fleet Street at that time. It is a copy of All Saints' church, The Pavement, York, and displays over the side entrance a contemporary statue of Queen Elizabeth I which once stood over Ludgate but was moved here after the demolition of the gateway in the eighteenth century. The carved heads of John Donne, poet and Dean of St Paul's Cathedral, and Izaak Walton, author of *The Compleat Angler*, can be seen on either side of the main entrance. Donne was once vicar here in the seventeenth century, and Walton lived in the parish and was a frequent worshipper at the church. John Donne was a convert to the Church of England from the Roman Catholic Church and served his curacy at St Mary's on Paddington Green before becoming vicar of St Dunstan's and Dean of St Paul's. The seventeenth-century clock standing to the right of the main entrance is from the former church and has two sparsely clad attendants who club out the hours to while away the time. William Cowper, the poet, wrote:

> *When Labour and when Dullness, club in hand,*
> *Like the two figures of St Dunstan's stand,*
> *Beating alternatively in measured time*
> *The clockwork tintinnabulum of rhyme,*
> *Exact and regular the sound will be,*
> *But such mere quarter strokes are not for me.*

Standing in the doorway, under Queen Elizabeth, are the figures of King Lud and his sons.

Today the church is host to several Orthodox churches, including the Coptic, Armenian and Romanian. There is also a Polish Roman Catholic shrine in the church.

King Lud and his sons are on the porch of St Dunstan-in-the-West.

Turn left from the church and walk down Fleet Street to the parish church of **St Bride (9)**, standing back on the right-hand side. Here is a remarkable survivor of both the Great Fire of 1666 and the Blitz of 1940 – a Tudor lectern. Before the restoration of the church in the 1950s extensive excavations were carried out by the Roman and Medieval London Excavation Council. The results can be seen in the crypt, which displays buildings from Roman times (a tessellated pavement) to the charnel houses of the seventeenth century. The east wall of the church, behind the main altar, is, in fact, flat but has been cunningly painted with a *trompe-l'oeil*, by Glyn Jones, to represent a round-ended apse. In the corner, opposite the north entrance, is a terracotta of a little girl by Margery Meggitt. It commemorates the first child of British parentage born in North America; her parents were parishioners and members of St Bride's.

Fleet Street leads to Ludgate Circus and Ludgate Hill, where the parish church of **St Martin within Ludgate (10)** acts as a foil for the cathedral at the top of the hill, with its leaden spire silhouetted against the sky holding its own against the massive dome of St Paul's. The font bears a Greek palindrome – a word or phrase which reads the same both ways. The translation reads 'Wash my sin, not my face only'. Over the font is a marble group of the

90

pelican in her piety, based on earlier representations of Christian interpretations of the sacrifice of Christ. Benjamin West, the first American President of the Royal Academy, painted the 'Ascension' which hangs on the east wall of the church. Close by can be seen three oil paintings by a Flemish artist depicting the three patron saints of the united benefice: St Mary Magdalene, St Martin and St Gregory.

Cross the roadway with care, turn left and walk up the hill to Creed Lane. This leads to Carter Lane and St Andrew's Hill. At the foot of the hill is the parish church of **St Andrew by the Wardrobe (11)**, which owes its suffix to its close proximity to the Great Wardrobe where the king's stores were housed. The church contains a number of items of furniture from other city churches. Its font and pulpit came from the demolished St Matthew's, Friday Street. From St Olave, Old Jewry, came the Royal Stuart coat of arms. They were originally a gift to that church from the rector of St Margaret, Lothbury. The weathervane on the church tower was designed by Wren for the now demolished church of St Michael, Bassishaw. Worship at the church is led from the organ, in the west gallery, that once was to be found in Lord Hatherton's Teddesley Hall, Stafford. Banners hanging in the church include those of the Worshipful Companies of Mercers, Blacksmiths and Parish Clerks, and the Worshipful Society of Apothecaries.

Leave St Andrew's by the south doorway. Descend the steps and pass under the gateway that is a memorial to Banister Fletcher, the

Guild banners hanging in St Andrew by the Wardrobe.

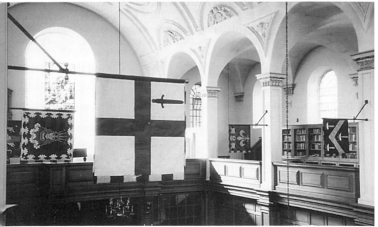

architect, who also wrote *A History of Architecture by the Comparative Method,* the 'bible' for architectural historians. At pavement level turn left and shortly on the opposite side of Queen Victoria Street is the church of **St Benet, Paul's Wharf (12).** Since 1877 this has been the Welsh Episcopalians' church, where services are held in the Welsh language every Sunday. Inigo Jones, the seventeenth-century architect, was buried in the pre-Fire church. The site of his grave is no longer marked but is said to have been in the north-east corner of the building. The church is seldom open, except at the time of service, when the wooden fittings given by Sir Llewellyn Jenkins, one of the chief ministers of Charles II, can be admired. From the nearby riverside wharf goods were unloaded for St Paul's Cathedral. It was also used by Sir Christopher Wren to examine the stone for the rebuilding of the cathedral.

Continue along Queen Victoria Street. To your right is all that is left of the church of **St Mary Somerset (13)**, the Wren tower, within which is a student's bed-sitting room! The remainder of the church was demolished in 1871, when it was sold for £10,000. John Stow, in his *Survay,* says that the suffix comes from Summers Hithe, after a local landowner of the dock nearby.

Finally, on the left in Queen Victoria Street, is the church of **St Nicholas Cole Abbey (14)**. No longer a parish church, it is now the Cole Abbey Presbyterian Church of Scotland. It houses a number of original carvings by Grinling Gibbons which survived the fires of 1940. Its weathervane, from the now demolished St Michael, Queenhithe, is a ship and reminds us that St Nicholas is the patron saint of sailors. The three east windows of the church, designed by Keith New, have as their theme 'Christ's Kingdom spreads throughout the world'. The suffix 'Cole Abbey' may come from a medieval benefactor, one Colby, or, more likely, from the 'cold harbour' which stood nearby, a shelter for vagrants in days gone by. In the early days of the underground railway system the church received the nickname St Mary Coal Hole. There was an air vent near the base of the tower through which steam and smoke from the engines would rise. A favourite ruse of the young men of the City was to get the young ladies to stand there – then it was not the steam that rose!

Mansion House underground station is a short distance from the church.

11
Inns and their curiosities

The original definition of an inn was a place where food, drink and lodgings could be obtained, whereas a tavern, strictly speaking, sold only drink, and woe betide the landlords of either who broke the law! Fitzstephen, writing in the twelfth century, said that London had two plagues, 'fire and drink', the former relating to the fact that most buildings were made of wood, and the latter being an accepted fact. He also tells of how young men in their cups would ring the bells of the local churches. Considering the number of churches at that time this must have caused quite a noise. At the medieval inn, where dormitory bedrooms were shared by both sexes, a bowl of soup cost a farthing, a bed a halfpenny, and a candle a farthing.

Scheduled as an ancient monument, the **Hoop and Grapes (1)** in Aldgate High Street, is one of the few pre-Fire buildings still in use. The previous building on the site, dating from the thirteenth century, was rebuilt early in the seventeenth century. Underneath there are sprawling cellars and passages, said to be those of the original building. Some of the passages are said to be the remains of tunnels that led to the Tower of London and were used by escaping prisoners or river pirates. Long before the advent of the telephone, the means of communication with the kitchen staff was through a 'lug-hole' in the wall; this curiously shaped hole allowed the landlord to speak to the staff, who would put their ears to the hole to hear the orders for meals. However, in more recent years this device has fallen into disuse.

After having been left at the church by his intended bride, Nathaniel Bentley, a 'gentleman of the eighteenth century', sealed up the room in which his wedding breakfast was to have taken place. The canny landlord of the Old Jerusalem tavern in Bishopsgate bought the room and incorporated it into his premises, renaming them **Dirty Dick's (2)**, after Bentley's nickname. Advertised as an ale and wine house, it is a popular venue.

At the foot of Tower Hill, opposite the entrance to the Tower of London, stands the **Tiger Tavern (3)**. Although rebuilt in the 1960s, it has a history that could fill a book on its own. In the upper bar a light switch on the wall illuminates a mummified cat, said to have been stroked by the young Princess Elizabeth, later Elizabeth I. While she was imprisoned in the Tower of London by her father Henry VIII and later her sister Queen Mary, she managed to escape from the dreary life of a prisoner by using an underground tunnel, said still to exist, and to have enjoyed a quiet drink or two in the

(Left) 'Dirty Dick's' in Bishopsgate and (right) the Olde Wine Shades in Martin Lane.

Tiger Tavern before returning to the Tower. An interesting ceremony takes place here every ten years when the beer is tested. The Lord Mayor of London and his retinue, including his own beer-taster, are duly received by mine host. The beer-taster, wearing leather breeches, sits on a stool on to which a sample of the beer has been poured and if he sticks to the stool then the beer is considered good, and all enjoy drinks on the house. The landlord has a garland placed around his neck and a laurel leaf bouquet is hung outside the door. The test has never been known to fail!

Built over three hundred years ago, surviving both the Great Fire and the Blitz, El Vino's **Olde Wine Shades (4)** in Martin Lane, off Cannon Street, only a stone's throw from where the Fire started, provides a quiet oasis in which to partake of one's favourite sherry or wine. Charles Dickens was a frequent visitor here and enjoyed

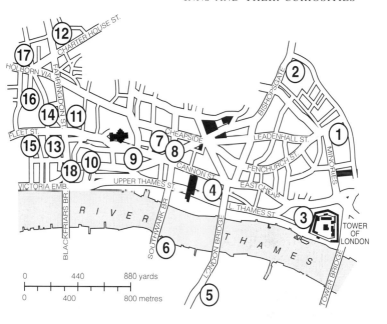

Inns and their curiosities

1. Hoop and Grapes, Aldgate High Street
2. Dirty Dick's, Bishopsgate
3. Tiger Tavern, Tower Hill
4. Olde Wine Shades, Martin Lane
5. George, Borough High Street
6. Anchor, Bankside
7. Williamson's Tavern, Bow Lane
8. Ye Olde Watling, Watling Street
9. Horn, Knightrider Street
10. Cockpit, St Andrew's Hill
11. Rumboe Tavern, Old Bailey
12. Castle, Cowcross Street
13. Bell, Fleet Street
14. Olde Cheshire Cheese, Fleet Street
15. Olde Cock Tavern, Fleet Street
16. Printer's Devil, New Fetter Lane
17. Mitre, Mitre Place
18. Black Friar, Queen Victoria Street

its atmosphere as much as visitors do today. Evidence of its age is confirmed by the date 1663 on a finely decorated lead cistern. Early documents refer to the building as being 'Sprague Shades', presumably recalling the original landlord. A relic of the time when the river was closer to the building than today is a blocked-up tunnel. Presumably this was used by the river pirates and the smugglers of former times.

When William Shakespeare was not imbibing at the Anchor on Bankside he could be found at the **George (5)** in Borough High Street, which is the only galleried inn left in London. Owned today by the National Trust, and therefore a protected building, it is only a shadow of its former self, as early in the twentieth century the other three sides of the inn-yard were pulled down to make way for a larger unloading bay for the railway company. This too has now been replaced by new buildings. One can still get to the upper rooms by way of the outside staircase.

Close by the Southwark side of Cannon Street railway bridge is the **Anchor (6)**, where the roadway which once ran in front of the building was removed during the redevelopment of the area. In

The George, Southwark, is the only galleried inn left in London.

addition a new riverside terrace has been created with a forecourt for the exclusive use of the patrons of the tavern. The present building replaces the one patronised by William Shakespeare between acts at the nearby Globe Theatre. Later, Dr Samuel Johnson, who obviously found compiling a dictionary of the English language thirsty work, came here. Did he, one wonders, drink the famous Russian Imperial Stout? This was specially brewed for the Empress of Russia in the eighteenth century: she drank it while eating oysters! There are tales of river pirates selling their booty to the barman, of escapes from the nearby Clink prison, and of the press gang, whose job it was to impress upon fit and hearty men the need to join the Navy. One of the river ferrymen overcharged Samuel Pepys, the diarist and Secretary to the Navy Office, for his journey across the river to the Anchor. Shortly afterwards the man found himself in the Navy!

In Groveland Court, a cul-de-sac alley off Bow Lane, is **Williamson's Tavern (7)**, which dates back to the eighteenth century when a Mr Williamson turned the house into a tavern or inn. Built on the site of the home of Sir John Falstaff, it had a large banqueting hall, said by some to be the original Mansion House, where a seventeenth-century Lord Mayor entertained William III and Queen Mary to dinner. Before dining, the royal guests presented the Lord Mayor with a pair of wrought-iron gates, which he accepted but then ordered to be taken outside. The Queen, angry at this, had them brought back again! Today they form the end piece to the alley. The Mansion House story is perpetuated by a room called the Mansion House Lounge. Also inside the house is an inscribed stone stating that it stands in the 'centre of London'. Evidence of an earlier house on the site was discovered during the rebuilding after the Second World War, when Roman tiles were found – they now form part of a fireplace.

Old photographs taken in the early part of the twentieth century show **Ye Olde Watling (8)** in Watling Street as a restaurant. Its original licence, once displayed at the bar, stated that a meal had to be ordered before a drink could be served. Today the tavern, very popular with city workers and tourists, is a pleasant oasis surrounded by the offices and shops of a very busy City.

Sandwiched between St Paul's Churchyard and Queen Victoria Street is Knightrider Street, the home of the **Horn public house (9)**, whose present building dates from the eighteenth century. It is first mentioned in the records in 1687 when several officers from the nearby College of Arms met there to discuss the rebuilding of the college. There is a distinct Dickensian atmosphere about the house but, alas, the sawdust has gone from the floor! Charles Dickens's bust smiles benignly from a shelf over the bar, and it is not hard to imagine members of the Pickwick Club frequenting the place in order to buy wine for the unlucky Mr Pickwick languishing in the Fleet Prison as a result of Mrs Bardell's breach of promise suit. While the area was being redeveloped in the 1980s the building was completely restored down to the last detail of the original.

You can almost hear the cocks crowing at the **Cockpit (10)** in St Andrew's Hill, for the interior shows what a cockpit looked like, while the pictures on the walls show many a proud old cock strutting about in triumph. The cockpit gallery is still there, although not accessible to members of the public.

Appropriately, the **Rumboe Tavern (11)** in the Old Bailey, being so near to the site of the former Newgate Prison, has decor to match its situation.

George IV was once attending a cock-fight in the vicinity of the **Castle (12),** Cowcross Street (close to Farringdon underground station), when he ran out of cash. Although the landlord did not recognise him, after a short argument he loaned him five pounds on the gold watch he had been given by his father, George III. Having won the bet for which he needed the money, he returned the money and redeemed the watch. The king offered the landlord a knighthood, which was refused, but he did accept the right to act as a pawnbroker. The inn sign incorporates three brass balls, the sign of a pawnbroker or money lender. A painting of the king's visit hangs on a wall of the bar.

There can be little doubt that rebuilding a city is thirsty work. The **Bell (13)**, with entrances in Fleet Street and Bride's Lane, was quickly rebuilt after the Fire to help sustain Wren's workmen.

Perhaps the most famous pub in Britain is the **Olde Cheshire Cheese (14)**, in Fleet Street; tourists from all over the world place it high on their list to be visited. It too was rebuilt soon after the Great Fire, but the site is much older and covers the cellars of the Abbots, later Bishops, of Peterborough. One of the haunts of Dr Samuel Johnson, it has attracted many other literary giants in its time. There is the story of a great fan of the Doctor who asked that his soup might be served in a dish used by Samuel Johnson. Doubtless with an eye to a possible tip, the waiter went away, found the most chipped dish on the premises and served the soup in it. The customer went away satisfied! The Olde Cheshire Cheese was also noted for its parrot, whose vocabulary of 'blue' language was surpassed by none, and connoisseurs from far and wide would come to listen to the bird. When it caught cold and died, its death was solemnly announced by the BBC and reported in newspapers all over the world, including the North China Star. It was duly stuffed and displayed on the bar, but now it seems to have flown away never to be seen again.

Although it moved to the other side of the street in the nineteenth century, the **Olde Cock Tavern (15)** in Fleet Street is still worth a visit to see the inn-sign from the former house, said to have been carved by Grinling Gibbons.

In 1957, presumably because at that time there were more printers than vintners in New Fetter Lane, the brewery changed the name of their pub from the Vintners to the **Printer's Devil (16)**. Named after a young boy, imp or devil, who did all the odd jobs about the printer's workshop, the pub houses a museum of the history of prints and printing on its walls. In addition to photographs, prints and samples of printers' work there are two working models of nineteenth-century printing presses.

A foundation stone on the outside of the **Mitre (17)**, Mitre Place – off Hatton Garden and leading to Ely Place – is dated 1547. As it is so near to the Bishop of Ely's town house there could well have been an inn on this corner long before that time. Inside, propping up one corner of the building, is a cherry-tree trunk around which Queen Elizabeth I is said to have danced, perhaps with her favour-

ite, Sir Christopher Hatton, joining in. For a time this tavern observed Cambridgeshire licensing hours, which was very convenient when they did not agree with the rest of London.

Built originally in the seventeenth century and rebuilt in 1903, the **Black Friar (18)**, at the end of Queen Victoria Street, is a lasting memorial to the Dominican friars (black friars) who lived here in the middle ages. Henry Poole RA was responsible for the interior decoration in the Art Nouveau style, depicting in marble, bronze, wood and glass the everyday happenings of the monastery. Do not miss the direction signs on the outside of the building pointing the way to the saloon bar.

The Black Friar has an Art Nouveau interior.

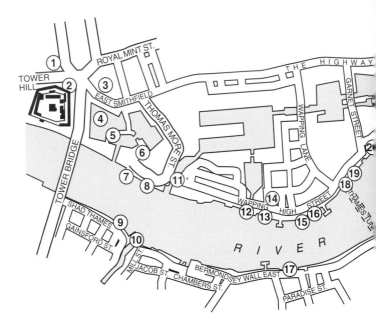

12. Curiosities of Docklands

At the **Tower Hill underground station (1)** there are two ways in
and out of the station. During the daytime there is an exit separate
from the booking office entrance. This is normally open only until
8 pm, after which the booking office serves as both entry and exit.

On leaving the daytime exit turn left and walk along to the
double flight of stairs. Halfway down on the left is a small green
open space. This space is opposite the booking hall entrance/exit.
Here can be seen the statue of the Emperor Trajan. It was discovered by the late Reverend 'Tubby' Clayton in a scrapyard while on
holiday. The Tower Hill Improvement Trust erected it here in 1980
as part of the landscape design. On the nearby wall can be seen
two-thirds of a Roman monumental inscription dedicated to
Classicianus who, was the procurator (or financial officer) from
AD 61 to 65 and had the unenviable task of pacifying the rebellious
tribe of the Iceni.

Continue the walk by descending the remainder of the flight of
stairs and pass through the tunnel under the roadway, where at the

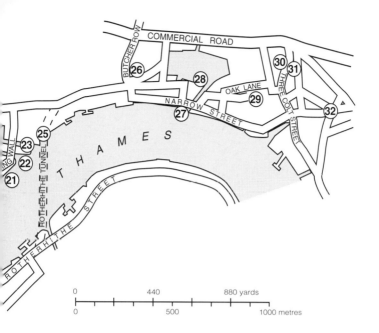

Curiosities of Docklands

1. Tower Hill station
2. Postern gateway
3. Cistercian abbey
4. London World Trade Centre
5. Coronarium chapel
6. Dickens Inn
7. HMS *President*
8. Thames Path
9. Design Museum
10. Butler's Wharf
11. Entrance to London Dock
12. Pierhead houses
13. Town of Ramsgate
14. St John's, Wapping
15. Metropolitan Police boatyard
16. Wapping New Stairs gardens
17. Angel public house
18. Captain Kidd
19. Wapping station
20. Two Suns public house
21. Prospect of Whitby
22. Thames Path
23. Entrance to Shadwell Basin
24. Shadwell Basin
25. King Edward Memorial Park
26. Royal Foundation of St Katharine
27. Grand Union Canal entrance
28. Limehouse Basin
29. Open space
30. St Anne, Limehouse
31. Five Bells and Bladebone
32. Westferry (DLR) station

The remains of the Abbey of St Mary Graces under an office block.

end are the ruins of a **postern gateway (2).** It is the only known example of a medieval postern gateway in the City wall. Judging by the masonry, it dates from the thirteenth century, at a time when the royal masons were making alterations to the nearby Tower of London. It was a multi-angular tower, complete with a portcullis, and with thin lancet slits that enabled the archer to fire his arrows at any enemy who might approach the City from its eastern boundaries.

From the postern turn left and walk along the pathway alongside the moat of the Tower of London. The path ends at the entrance to another tunnel that leads to a third one. Follow this to the end and walk up the steps, through the gate, if open, to find the ruins of a **Cistercian abbey (3)** – the Abbey of St Mary Graces. Founded in 1345 by Edward III, it became, at the time of the Dissolution of the Monasteries, one of the richest abbeys in England. In spite of an urgent plea from the Lord Mayor of London, William Forman, to Henry VIII, it was dissolved in 1538. The site was then used as a victualling yard by the Royal Navy until 1740, after which it was used as a government warehouse, and finally in 1790 as the site for the 'new' Royal Mint. In 1968 the Mint moved to south Wales, and the site was developed as office accommodation. It was during this latter stage that the abbey was excavated and these ruins were left open to public view. If the gates to the gardens are locked, particularly at weekends, the ruins can be viewed from the highway side of the building.

Return to the last tunnel and cross under the highway to the end of the second tunnel. Turn to the left, walk across the small bridge over the water and alongside the **London World Trade Centre (4).** Between the Centre and International House is a modern amphitheatre and nearby is the first dock making up the small complex that now constitutes the St Katharine Docks. Up to the sixteenth century the site was occupied by the Royal Foundation of St Katharine, a monastic establishment founded by Queen Matilda as a hospice. The Foundation still flourishes in Butcher Row, Stepney. The docks today often house a number of the famous sailing barges that once were to be seen plying for hire on the river.

To the left is a walkway that leads around the dock to the Ivory House. Completed in 1854 to the designs of Philip Hardwick, the house with its cast-iron columns and attractive brickwork above has been converted into offices, shops and comfortable living quarters. It was built to house the ivory trade's wares but now it overlooks the marina.

Across the water is the **Coronarium chapel (5),** a circular inter-denominational chapel. On the feast day of St Katharine (25th November) a short service is held in the chapel and children from a local church school attend.

On the other side of the dock from the Ivory House is the **Dickens Inn (6),** converted into an eating and drinking place from an eighteenth-century warehouse. Opened in 1976 by the great-grandson of Charles Dickens, it has become a place of unusual interest. Its ground floor serves only real ales, with not a bottle in sight, while the upper floors provide food.

Continue left and leave the Dock and walk along to St Katharine's

St Katharine's Dock.

Way, where, on the right-hand side, is **HMS President (7)** and the London Division of the Royal Navy Reserve. The ship of the same name used to be moored in King's Reach, opposite the Temple, but this has now been sold and is used for purposes other than training for the Royal Navy. The 'ship' is not opened to members of the general public.

Just beyond number 84 there is a signpost pointing the way to the **Thames Path (8)**, open to the public between the hours of 8 am and 11 pm. Follow the direction of the sign and wander along the riverside. The developments on the opposite side of the river include the **Design Museum (9)**, 'the first of its kind in the world'. In its exhibitions the museum explores the role of modern designs from mass production to the present day. Most of the warehouses on the Southwark bank of the river opposite have been converted into housing and none better than those on **Butler's Wharf (10)** lining the sides of St Saviour's Dock.

At the end of the path turn left, where on the right is the blocked-in entrance to the **London Dock (11)**. Cross over the roadway, Wapping High Street, where the remains of the dock have been filled with water. Keep on the same side of the roadway and walk towards Wapping Basin and Pierhead.

This marks the way into the western section of London Dock, which, like the other entrance to the dock, has been filled in and makes a pleasant oasis amidst the housing. On the right-hand side of the roadway is **Pierhead (12)**, where, at the river end, is the

Pierhead has two splendid terraces of Georgian houses either side of a grassed square.

former Dock Master's House. All the houses here were built between 1811 and 1812.

On the same side of the road are the **Town of Ramsgate public house (13)** and Wapping Old Stairs. Previously shown on maps as the Red Cow, Wapping High Street, in deference to the colour of a barmaid's hair, it was renamed the Town of Ramsgate after being adopted by the Ramsgate fishermen who used to sell their fish from Old Wapping Stairs at the side of the house. It was on these steps that 'Bloody' Judge Jeffreys was caught disguised as a sailor when trying to escape to Hamburg. Recognised, he was taken to the Tower of London, where he died of 'wasting disease'. He was later buried, secretly, in the church of St Mary, Aldermanbury. When the church was being taken down to be rebuilt at Westminster College, University of Fulton, Missouri, in the United States of America the grave was discovered. The site has not been marked.

Sailors found guilty of crime on the high seas were sentenced to death by being washed over by three tides at this point of the river. The effect of the water was to bloat the bodies, hence the saying 'What a wopper', meaning somebody executed in the river near here. The tavern has a grisly history, with tunnels leading towards the Tower of London, and a garden that was once used as a hanging dock for petty thieves. A replica gallows adorns the garden. The pirate Captain Kidd is said to haunt the house.

Opposite is a disused churchyard, now an open space. Across Scandrett Road is the parish church of **St John, Wapping (14)**. The church, built in 1756, replaced a chapel of ease that had been built here in 1617 and was consecrated by the Bishop of Rochester, Zachariah Pearce, 'By Commission of the Bishop of London' (Thomas Sherlock), in 1760. The architect was Joel Johnson, who was also associated with the building of the London Hospital in Whitechapel, and who with his father took several building leases on the Harley Estate in Marylebone. The Reverend Francis Willis MD, rector here at one time, attended George III during his first bout of mental illness. The whole area of Wapping suffered extensively during the Second World War and the church was bombed, leaving only the tower; this was restored at a later date.

Next to the church are the buildings of the former St John's Wapping Church School, founded in 1695, and rebuilt in 1790. Over the doorway are the figures of a boy and a girl with inscriptions noting that the school was for fifty girls and sixty boys. The buildings have now been converted into private housing.

A few yards from the school in 1834 was born the butcher and impostor Arthur Orton, alias Thomas Castro, also known as the Tichborne Claimant. While living in Australia he met Sir Joseph Tichborne, the eleventh baronet, on whose death in 1866 Orton

Figures over the entrance of the former church school in Wapping.

persuaded the wife of the tenth baronet that he was her eldest son who had been presumed drowned at sea off the coast of America in 1854. On his return to England in 1866 he contested the claim of the twelfth baronet to the title but after over one hundred days in court the case collapsed. Afterwards Orton was charged with perjury, found guilty after a second trial that lasted one hundred and eighty days, and sentenced to seven years hard labour. On his release in 1884, he openly confessed to the imposture. He died in 1898 and was buried in Paddington Cemetery.

Just past the church tower, on the corner of Scandrett Street, named after the Reverend John Scandrett, rector of St John's from 1900 to 1908, and Green Bank is the former Turk's Head public house. Walk along Green Bank, where on the right is the modern Roman Catholic church of St Patrick, and opposite another open space complete with playground equipment. At Dundee Street turn right and return to Wapping High Street, at the junction of which is St John's Warehouse, now converted into private housing.

Opposite is the **Metropolitan Police boatyard (15)**, which serves the nearby Wapping Police Station.

From **Wapping New Stairs gardens (16)** the wide vista of the river includes Rotherhithe on the opposite bank with the **Angel (17)**, 'a sixteenth century riverside pub' frequented by the diarist Samuel Pepys. He records visiting the tavern after having walked over the fields from the naval dockyard. He was Secretary to the Navy Office at Deptford. The tower and spire of the parish church of St Mary, Rotherhithe, are to the left, rebuilt in the eighteenth century. The former village of Rotherhithe was among a number of riverside villages that were deeply engaged in shipbuilding in the past. To the far left is the second tallest tower block in Europe, Canary Wharf, rising 800 feet (244 metres) above the Thames and

London. These gardens are a favourite place for local anglers fishing for eels. From the riverside can be seen the boats and landing stage of the river police.

On leaving the gardens turn right and shortly pass the Wapping Police Station, now the home of the Thames Division Headquarters of the Metropolitan Police Force.

Continue along Wapping High Street to the **Captain Kidd (18)**, where the bars and restaurants overlook the river. Kidd was a notorious sea captain who was commissioned in 1696 to suppress pirates but instead joined them. He was finally caught in New England and sent back to London, where, in 1701, he was hanged at Execution Dock close to Wapping Old Stairs. The various bars have names such as The Gallows and all have fine views across the river. Brewhouse Lane on the left-hand side of the roadway is a reminder of the number of breweries that once stood along this stretch of the river.

Wapping station (19), on the right, was opened in 1869 as Wapping & Shadwell and renamed Wapping in 1876. Wapping was linked with Rotherhithe, on the opposite side of the river, by the world's first underwater tunnel. It had been opened in March 1843 as a tunnel for foot passengers. It was designed by Isambard Kingdom Brunel and intended to be used by vehicular traffic but there was insufficient money to build the necessary ramps and so the scheme was abandoned. In the 1860s it was bought by the East London Railway Company and converted for use by its trains in 1884. At the platform level the twin horseshoe-shaped tunnels can be seen. The journey by train along the 400 yard (366 metre) tunnels takes only a few minutes.

At the end of Wapping High Street is Garnet Street, where turn left, and on the next corner, Wapping Wall, is the former **Two Suns (20)** public house. Built in the style of seventeenth-century Dutch architecture, its frontage has an ornate upper storey.

At the end of Wapping Wall is one of the oldest riverside public houses, the **Prospect of Whitby (21)**; on the front of the building is a board with the date *c.*1520. It was originally called the Devil's Tavern, doubtless from its associations with the smugglers and thieves who used to haunt this stretch of the river. Samuel Pepys visited the house a number of times. Later 'Bloody' Judge Jeffreys came here to watch the river executions, and in the nineteenth century Charles Dickens is said to have used the Prospect as the Six Jolly Fellowship Porters in *Our Mutual Friend*. By Dickens's time the name had been altered from the Devil's Tavern to the Prospect of Whitby, because a ship named the *Prospect* and registered at Whitby in North Yorkshire was often moored alongside the tavern.

To the side of the building is another stretch of the **Thames Path**

The famous 'Prospect of Whitby' was originally called the Devil's Tavern.

(22), leading round to the **entrance (23)** to **Shadwell Basin (24)**. 'Shadwell' is derived from the local St Chad's Well, the site of which is unknown. The path leads in turn to a bridge over the dock mouth. Cross over the roadway to see the basin. Modern housing surrounds it and from here the parish church of St Paul, Shadwell, can be seen over the tops of the houses. With the spread of London in the seventeenth century a number of small hamlets had chapels of ease built to serve the local community. In 1656 one was built between the Ratcliffe Highway and the river. With the further growth of population it was rebuilt in 1669 as the parish church of Shadwell. Dedicated to St Paul, the patron saint of the London diocese, it was the last church to be built in the area for thirty years. During the eighteenth century it became known as the sea captains' church. Nearly two hundred names of ships' captains and their wives are recorded in the parish registers between 1730 and 1790. Captain James Cook's son was baptised here in 1728. The present church was built in the early nineteenth century, with money from the Waterloo Churches Fund, voted by Parliament as a thank-offering for the deliverance of the nation from the threat of invasion and conquest by Napoleon.

Return to the right-hand side of the roadway and follow the next portion of the Thames Path to **King Edward VII Memorial Park (25)**. Formerly the site of a fish market and a 'few acres of slums', the park was officially opened in 1922. Gone are the poor housing, fish market and riverside warehouses, and in their place a fine stretch of the river has been opened up for all to enjoy. Standing close to the riverside is the ventilation shaft of the Rotherhithe Tunnel. The tunnel carries road traffic from a point in Commercial

Road to Rotherhithe. On the park side of the shaft there is a ceramic memorial tablet:

This tablet is in memory of
Sir Hugh Willoughby, Stephen Borough,
William Borough, Sir Martin Frobisher
and other navigators who, in the latter
half of the sixteenth century, set sail
from this reach of the River Thames, near
Ratcliff Cross
to explore the Northern Seas

Erected by the London County Council 1922.

Little is known about Sir Hugh Willoughby except for his unfortunate fate. He and his crew died of the cold and scurvy while on their voyage to 'discover regions, dominions, islands and places unknown'. The account of the voyage was published by the Hakluyt Society in 1903. Leave the park by the gate alongside the riverside.

Leave the riverside by way of the Free Trade Wharf and on reaching the Highway turn right and walk along to the traffic lights. On the opposite side of the roadway is Butcher Row, one of the oldest thoroughfares in this part of London.

Here is the latest home of the **Royal Foundation of St Katharine in Ratcliffe (26)**, founded in 1147 by Matilda, queen of King Stephen, as a spiritual centre, a place of learning and a means of hospitality and social help. It has had a continuous history of over eight hundred years and was the only religious foundation to survive the traumas of the Reformation and the Dissolution of the Monasteries. Today under its Master the foundation continues to work for the East End of London. The main building dates from the eighteenth century, when it was built for a wealthy sugar merchant, Matthew Whiting, and later became the vicarage for the now demolished parish church of St James Ratcliffe. In the modern chapel is a beautiful collection of fourteenth-century choir stalls complete with misericords. The walls of both the former dining room and the drawing room are painted and include Claude Vernet's 'Sun Rising in the Mist'. Over the entrance a blue plaque records the residence here of Father John Grosser, 1890 to 1966, priest and social reformer.

Return to the Highway and rejoin the Thames Path, which leads into Narrow Street, and walk along to the bridge over the entrance to the **Grand Union Canal (27)**. Here the canal ends its journey from Birmingham, having passed through Paddington, Regent's Park and St Pancras. On the latter stages of its journey the canal was built as the Regent's Canal. The next bridge crosses the Limehouse Cut, which enables barges to use the river Lea without having to pass round the Isle of Dogs.

Walk up Northey Street, where can be found the headquarters of the Cruising Association. There are small groups of houses, between which the **Limehouse Basin (28)** can be seen. The basin is now a marina and various types of boats are moored here, either permanently or temporarily.

At the far end of the street there is an **open space (29)**, from which another view of the basin can be enjoyed. Leave by the far side gate and walk along to Newell Street (previously called Church Row). It was in Church Row that one of Charles Dickens's godfathers, a naval rigger, whom he used to visit regularly, lived. Later Dickens incorporated his impressions of the area in his writings. Here lived Captain Cuttle and Mrs MacStinger in *Dombey and Son*. He visited Limehouse when writing *Our Mutual Friend* in 1863. He left a clear picture of the Grapes public house, an alternative location for the Six Jolly Fellowship Porters.

A short side street leads to the parish church of **St Anne, Limehouse (30)**, 'a pleasant church in a pleasant garden'. It is another of the Nicholas Hawksmoor's churches built under the eighteenth-century Act of Parliament for the provision of fifty new churches in and around the capital, of which only a dozen were ever built. The west tower is 130 feet (40 metres) high and houses the highest church clock in London. Unfortunately for the parishioners, on Good Friday 1850 a disastrous fire gutted the building. A careful restoration by Philip Hardwick and John Morris resulted in a perfect replica. The question 'What is that pyramid doing in the churchyard ?' is still unsolved. One suggestion is that it was either the original top of the tower or had been intended to be the top of the tower. Nobody knows!

On the opposite side of the churchyard in Three Colts Street is the **Five Bells and Bladebone public house (31)**; the five bells are those used to denote the end of the lunchtime session in the docks. The site had been previously occupied by an abattoir and during the erection of the building various bones and knives were discovered. Appropriately the decor of the house reflects the docks and Docklands and includes both a bell and a bladebone over the bar. At the end of the street is Commercial Road, where turn right and follow the roadway by way of West India Dock Road to **Westferry station** on the Docklands Light Railway **(32).**

From the station the railway will quickly take you either to Tower Gateway station or to Bank station. To explore the area around Canary Wharf the railway will take you into the heart of the development.

Index